Daniel Maslen

THE EFFECTS OF SPIRI

THE EFFECTS OF SPIRITUAL DEVELOPMENT

*A cycle of ten lectures
given at The Hague from 20 to 29 March 1913*

Rudolf Steiner

translated by
A. H. Parker

RUDOLF STEINER PRESS
35 PARK ROAD LONDON NW1 6XT

First published privately in English with the title *The Effect of Occult Development upon the Bodies and the Self of Man*

Second Edition with the title *The Effect of Occult Development upon the Self and the Sheaths of Man* by Rudolf Steiner Publishing Company, London, and Anthroposophic Press, New York, 1945

Third Edition (new translation) by Rudolf Steiner Press, London 1978

Translated from shorthand reports unrevised by the lecturer. The German text is published under the title: *Welche Bedeutung hat die okkulte Entwicklung des Menschen für seine Hüllen und sein Selbst?* (Bibl. No. 145). This English translation is published in agreement with the *Rudolf Steiner-Nachlassverwaltung*, Dornach, Switzerland.

© Rudolf Steiner Press, London, 1978

ISBN 0 85440 319 1 (cased)
ISBN 0 85440 320 5 (paperback)

Printed in Great Britain by
The Camelot Press Ltd, Southampton

CONTENTS

LECTURE ONE   20 March 1913   7
Influences of anthroposophical life on the sheaths of man

LECTURE TWO   21 March 1913   19
The inner experience of foodstuffs

LECTURE THREE   22 March 1913   35
The evolution of man's senses in past, present and future. The effect of esoteric development on the temperaments

LECTURE FOUR   23 March 1913   50
The differentiated experience of the etheric

LECTURE FIVE   24 March 1913   66
The transformation of judgement, feeling and willing

LECTURE SIX   25 March 1913   81
The legend of Paradise and the legend of the Holy Grail

LECTURE SEVEN   26 March 1913   96
The struggle of astrality with egoism. Amfortas and Parzifal

LECTURE EIGHT   27 March 1913   113
The Paradise Imagination. The Guardian of the Threshold. The story of Cain and Abel

LECTURE NINE   28 March 1913   127
Centaur and sphinx. Lucifer and Ahriman. The appearance of Christ in the etheric sphere

LECTURE TEN   29 March 1913   140
The etheric body records cosmic history. The twelve members of the cosmos through which the Hierarchies speak

LECTURE ONE

The Hague, 20 March 1913

I propose to speak to you on a subject which may be important for many at the present time, important for all those who in some way endeavour to avoid a theoretical approach to spiritual science, but who endeavour to open their hearts and minds to spiritual science so that it becomes an essential ingredient of their lives, something that enters into their whole life. It is important not only for the genuine initiate, but also for those who wish to imbue their soul life with anthroposophical thoughts, to learn something of the modifications which the whole human being undergoes when he practises the exercises given in my book *Knowledge of the Higher Worlds* or sketched more briefly in the second part of *Occult Science – An Outline*, or even when one adopts wholeheartedly anthroposophical thoughts. When cultivated seriously, either esoterically or exoterically, Anthroposophy produces a certain modification in the whole organisation of man. It can be confidently affirmed that one becomes a different person through Anthroposophy; the whole structure of man's being is transformed. The physical body, the etheric body, the astral body and the true Self of man are transformed in a certain way when he really assimilates Anthroposophy. I propose to discuss in turn the modifications which the human sheaths undergo under the influence of esotericism or through the exoteric study of Anthroposophy when undertaken seriously.

It is particularly difficult to speak of the modifications of the physical body for the simple reason that, although these modifications of the physical body at the beginning of the esoteric life are important and significant, they are also often indistinct and trifling. Important and significant modifications occur in the physical body, but they are imperceptible externally to any kind of external knowledge for the simple reason that the physical body is that which inwardly is least under man's control and because dangers would arise immediately if esoteric exercises or anthroposophical activity were to be directed in such a way that the modifications of the physical body exceeded the measure of what the neophyte can fully control. The modifications of the physical body are kept within certain limits; but it is important, however, that the neophyte should know something of these modifications, that he should have a clear understanding of them.

If we wish to characterise briefly the modifications which the physical body undergoes under the conditions just mentioned we must say: this physical body becomes at first more mobile and inwardly more active. What do we mean by "more mobile"? Now in the normal life of man the individual organs of the physical body are connected with each other in a certain way. The activities of these individual organs are inter-related. When the pupil takes up esotericism or Anthroposophy seriously, the individual organs become more independent of one another. The total life of the physical body is to a certain extent modified and the individual life of the organs is reinforced. Although the extent of the modification of the total life of the body and the reinforcement of the individual life of the organs is extremely small, we must say, however, that, under the influence of esotericism and Anthroposophy, the heart, brain and spinal cord especially, all organs, in fact, become more autonomous, more active and more independent of one another, they become inwardly more mobile. In technical language, the organs pass from a state of stable equilibrium to a state of more unstable equilibrium. It is well to be aware of this fact because, when the pupil perceives something of this state of disbalance in his organs he is inclined to attribute it to illness or indisposition. He is not accustomed to feel the mobility, the independence of his organs; he becomes aware of, he feels them only when they do not function normally. He now feels —

though imperceptibly at first – that the organs are independent of each other and he may take this as a sign of indisposition or illness. You see therefore that we must be careful when dealing with the physical body. Clearly, what may be in the one case the onset of illness, may be, in another case, simply the attendant phenomenon of the inner life of Anthroposophy. Each case, therefore, must be judged individually; but what is achieved under these circumstances through the practice of Anthroposophy is quite in accordance with the normal course of human evolution. In earlier times of evolution the individual organs were still more dependent upon each other than they are today in external life and in future they will become increasingly more autonomous. Just as the student of Anthroposophy must always, in the different spheres of life and knowledge, anticipate the stages of development which will only be attained in future by the whole of mankind, so too he must so to speak accept, in conformity with this stage of development, that his organs become more independent of each other. This modification may show itself almost imperceptibly in the individual organs and organic systems.

I will give you a characteristic example. You are all familiar with this phenomenon: when a man has grown roots, when his profession offers little opportunity for travel he becomes (to some extent) tied to his native soil. If you go into the country you will find that the peasant is much more attached to his native soil and climate than the townsman who often spends his holidays in the country, and if for some reason or other he is transplanted to another region or climate, he finds it difficult to acclimatise himself; he never loses his longing for his native soil, he feels a nostalgia that is often impossible to overcome. This is simply a reminder that man – and this we can usually perceive when he moves to another region – must adapt his whole organism to this region and to this new climate. Normally this adaptation takes place in the whole organism. Everything is affected, everything is involved when we leave the plains for the mountains or when we move to a distant country. In the initiate, in the serious student of Anthroposophy it is noticeable that the whole organism is no longer involved, but that the blood system is isolated and that the circulation of the blood is insulated, as it were, from the rest of the organism and when the pupil moves from one district to another the circulation of the blood is more seriously affected. Someone who develops a certain sensitivity to these things can detect in fact a change in the pulsation of the blood in the way the pulse beats when he moves from one place to another. Whilst in the ordinary person the necessary acclimatisation makes heavy demands upon the nervous system, in the initiate and the serious student of Anthroposophy the nervous system will be little affected. Thanks to the anthroposophical inner life the nervous system is insulated from the blood system which becomes more sensitive to the influences of climate and soil; the nervous system on the other hand becomes more independent.

If you wish to have proofs of this fact you must look for them where they are to be found most easily, namely, when you find yourself in a similar position, when you yourself move to another district. Try to observe yourself carefully and you will find confirmation of this occult fact. It is extremely important to bear this fact in mind, simply because this fact is gradually transformed into a very definite faculty of perception. He who has accepted anthroposophical teachings is aware of the character of a foreign town by the pulsation of his blood. There is no need for further investigation; he can tell by the pulsation of his blood that the regions of the earth are different from one another. The nervous system, on the other hand, is insulated from the whole organism in a different way. He who studies Anthroposophy in the way I have indicated will gradually perceive that he is aware of the difference between the four seasons, especially of the difference between summer and winter in a totally different way from the ordinary man of today. For the most part the latter only feels in his own physical body the difference of temperature. He who has assimilated Anthroposophy in the way already indicated, perceives not only the difference in temperature, but, in addition he has a particular experience in his nervous system, so that, for example, he finds it easier in summer to cultivate certain thoughts that are connected with the physical brain, rather than in winter. Not that it is impossible to think certain thoughts in winter; but one can see quite clearly that it is easier to do so in summer than in winter, that they flow more easily in summer. We can observe that in winter thoughts more easily become abstract, whilst in summer they more easily become clear and vivid. The reason for this is that the nervous system, the instrument intended for the physical plane, vibrates delicately in harmony with the change of seasons, and vibrates inwardly more independently of the whole organism than is normally the case.

A fundamental modification, however, takes place in the physical body; we begin – and this may assume most disquieting forms – to be more aware of our physical body than before. The body becomes more sensitive to the soul life, it becomes more difficult to tolerate. It is extremely difficult to explain this clearly. Imagine a glass of water in which salt has been dissolved, thus producing an opaque liquid. Suppose that, in man's normal condition, his etheric body, astral body and Self are this liquid and that his physical body is dissolved like the salt. Now allow the liquid to cool down. The salt will slowly crystallise out and become heavier, because it has become independent. In the same way the physical body "crystallises out" of the whole structure of the four members of the human being. It contracts, though only to a small extent. This must be taken quite literally, it contracts in a certain sense but you must not exaggerate the extent of contraction. There is no need to fear that through anthroposophical development man will become excessively wrinkled. This shrivelling is a process of inner densification. In consequence the body is more difficult to tolerate than before; it is felt to be less mobile. And moreover the other members are now more flexible. The body of which one was not aware when it was perfectly healthy and which one quite naturally addressed as "I", is now felt as something within which has seemingly become heavier and which one begins to feel in its totality. And in particular one begins to be aware of all those organs in the physical body which, from the outset, lead a certain independent existence. Here we touch upon a question which can only be fully understood in this connection, the question of meat diet. I have no wish to proselytise, of course, I only wish to present the facts.

Since we are dealing with the physical body we must first describe the nature of animal food, plant food and of food in general. All this is intended as an interlude in the discussion of the influences of anthroposophical life upon the sheaths of man. We may describe it as the restoration, the regeneration of the physical body through the ingestion of substances he receives from without. The relation of man to his food is only properly understood when we bear in mind the relationship of man to the other kingdoms of nature. The plant kingdom, as a kingdom of life, brings the inorganic substances, the mineral substances, to a certain stage of organisation. In order that the plant may develop it is taken for granted that the lifeless substances as if in a living laboratory are worked up in a certain way and are brought to a certain stage of organisation. In the plant we have a living organism which brings the lifeless products of nature to a certain stage of development. Now man is so organised physically that he is in a position to continue this process of development from the point where the plant left off, so that the higher human organism arises when man develops further that which the plant has already brought to a certain stage. Things are designed with such economy that when a man plucks a leaf or gathers an apple and eats it, we are aware of the perfect continuity. That is an example of the most perfect continuity. Were things so designed that they followed the most natural course, we might say: the most natural course would be for man to continue the process of development from the point where the plant left off, i.e. to take the organs of the plant as he finds them externally and from that point to develop them further within himself. That would provide a straight line of development which would not be interrupted anywhere or in any way, from the lifeless substance up to a certain stage in the development of the plant and from there to the human organism.

LECTURE ONE

Let us now take the extreme case of a man who eats animal flesh. In the animal we have a living being which takes the process of organisation further than the plant, to a certain stage beyond the plant organisation, so that we can now say of the animal that it continues the process of organisation of the plant. Let us now suppose that a man eats animal flesh. The following then occurs: he no longer needs to use the inner forces which were necessary in order to digest plant food. If he had been obliged to organise the foodstuffs from the point where the plant left off, he would have had to use certain forces. These remain unused when he eats animal flesh, for the animal has brought the organisation of the plant to a higher stage, and man need only begin the development of his organisation from this stage. We can say therefore that man does not continue the work of organisation from the point at which he could have done; he leaves forces that are in him unused and continues the work of organisation later. He allows the animal to take over a part of the work which he would have had to do had he eaten plant food. Now the well-being of an organ does not consist in working as little as possible, but in activating all its forces. When a man eats only plant food he stimulates the forces which develop organic activities; when he eats animal food he fails to make use of these forces and behaves like the man who says: I will do without my left arm; I will bind it up so that it cannot be used. Thus when he eats animal flesh he imprisons the forces which he would normally call upon if he were to eat plant food. He condemns therefore a certain sum of forces within his organism to inactivity with the result that the organisations in question which would otherwise be active lie fallow and are crippled and become hardened. When a man eats animal flesh therefore, he kills, or at least paralyses a part of his organism. And that part of his organism which thus becomes hardened, he carries with him throughout his life as a foreign body. In his normal life he is unaware of this foreign body, but when his organism becomes inwardly more mobile and his organs become more independent of one another, as occurs in anthroposophical training, then his physical body which moreover already feels ill at ease, begins to feel still more uneasy because it has now a foreign body within it.

Now as I have already said, I have no wish to proselytise, I simply wish to state the truth. And we shall learn of other effects of animal food; and on this occasion we shall be obliged to discuss this subject in further detail. Thus progress in the anthroposophical life gradually produces a kind of disgust for animal food. Not that it is necessary to forbid animal food to anthroposophists, for through the development of a healthy instinctive life one gradually rejects animal food, one loses the taste for it. And this is far better than becoming a vegetarian in the name of some abstract principle. Best of all, however, is when Anthroposophy develops naturally in man a kind of disgust and abhorrence of animal food. To abstain from animal food for other reasons is of little value in terms of what may be called man's higher development. We can say therefore that animal food produces in man something that the physical body feels as a burden. Such are the facts of the case from an occult point of view.

Let us now look at this question from a different point of view. Let us take the case of alcohol. The relation of man to alcohol is also modified when he takes up Anthroposophy and makes spiritual science an integral part of his life. Alcohol is something quite special in the kingdom of nature. It proves to be not only a dead weight in the human organism, but acts directly as a counter-force on the organism. When we observe the plant we find that it develops its organisation up to a certain point, whilst the vine develops beyond this point. What the other plants reserve solely for the germ, that is, all the vegetal germinating power which is usually reserved for the germ alone and does not enter into the rest of the plant, this vegetative power in the grape flows in a certain way into the fruit pulp as well, so that through what is known as fermentation, through the transformation of that which enters into the grape, of that which has been brought to maximum activity, in the grape itself, something is produced which attains a power within the plant which can only be compared occultly to the power which the Ego of man has over the blood. Thus, in the making of wine and in the production of alcohol, there is created in another kingdom of nature that which man must create when he works upon his blood from out of his Ego.

We know that there is a close relationship between the Ego and the blood. This is expressed externally by the fact that when the Ego feels shame a blush suffuses the face; when the Ego is afraid or anxious the person turns pale. This normal action of the Ego upon the blood is comparable occultly to the effect which is produced when the vegetal process becomes retroactive, so that what is contained in the fruit pulp of the grape, the grape juice, is transformed into alcohol. As we have said, the Ego must normally produce in the blood – speaking occultly, not chemically – a process similar to that which is produced (in the grape) by the reversal of the process of organisation, by the purely chemical action of this process when alcohol is produced. Consequently alcohol introduces into the organism something which from the outside acts like the Ego upon the blood. That is to say, when we consume alcohol we introduce a counter-Ego, an Ego which directly opposes the deeds of our spiritual Ego. Thus, alcohol acts upon the blood in the same way as the Ego acts upon the blood. Hence an inner war is unleashed; and we condemn to impotence everything that proceeds from the Ego when we consume alcohol which is the antagonist of the Ego. That is the situation from the occult point of view. He who abstains from alcohol ensures for himself the possibility to work freely upon his blood from out of his Ego; he who drinks alcohol behaves like someone who wishes to demolish a wall and hammers on the one side, at the same time placing on the other side people who hammer in opposition to him. In the same way the consumption of alcohol eliminates the activity of the Ego on the blood.

Hence, he who makes Anthroposophy the corner-stone of his life feels the action of alcohol in his blood as a direct attack upon his Ego, and it is therefore quite natural that a true spiritual development only comes easily if one avoids this conflict. From this example we see how that which is normally present becomes *perceptible* to the anthroposophist when he is aware that the normal equilibrium in his physical body is modified.

In many other respects the different organs and organic systems of the physical organisation become independent, the spinal cord and the brain especially become much more independent of each other. Tomorrow we shall speak further on the subject of nutrition and the occult physiology of nutrition. Today, however, I propose to keep more to the theme of the independence of the organs! This independence of the spinal chord from the brain may come to light because, when man's soul is permeated with Anthroposophy, he is able gradually to feel that his organism is achieving greater independence. This, in its turn, may lead to very unpleasant situations. It is all the more necessary therefore that one should be aware of this. It may happen, for example, that whilst one normally has oneself under control, the more advanced student suddenly finds himself saying things which he never really intended to say. He is walking along the road; suddenly he notices that he has let slip a word, a favourite expression of his which he would have refrained from saying if he had not experienced this dissociation of the spinal chord from the brain. What is usually inhibited becomes simply reflex action as a result of this dissociation. In the brain certain parts become independent of other parts; the inner parts of the brain, for example, become more independent of the outer parts surrounding them, whilst in normal life the inner and outer parts work more in harmony. This is shown by the fact that for the esotericist or the true anthroposophist abstract thinking becomes more difficult than it was before and gradually meets with resistance on the part of the brain. The budding anthroposophist finds it easier to think imaginatively than to think abstractly.

This is very soon apparent in many ardent anthroposophists. They show a predilection for anthroposophical activity alone; they like to read Anthroposophy, to reflect on anthroposophical subjects, not only because they are ardent anthroposophists, but because they find it easier to be at home in more spiritual ideas or conceptions. These more spiritual ideas, in so far as the physical plane is concerned, claim the attention of the middle parts of the brain, whilst abstract thinking claims the other parts. Hence the aversion of many over-zealous anthroposophists from abstract thought and abstract knowledge. And this again is why certain anthroposophists realise with some regret that, whilst formerly they could easily think in abstract terms, they now find it more difficult.

Thus the separate organs become relatively more active and independent, and even certain parts of these organs become more active and independent. From this you can see that something new, as it were, must arise in many who experience this transformation. Formerly, it was benevolent nature which, without his cooperation, brought his organs into the right harmonious relationship; now, these organs are becoming more independent, they are more loosely related to one another and he must have the inner strength to re-establish harmony amongst them. This harmony of the various organs is attained through a sound study of Anthroposophy because it continually emphasises everything that increases the dominion of man over his organs which have become independent. Remember, therefore, how often people have emphasised – and this plays a large part in our anthroposophical literature – that Anthroposophy is terribly difficult! When I learned that my book *Theosophy* was too difficult for beginners I often had to give the same answer: it ought not to be easier, for had it been made easier people would obviously have accepted certain anthroposophical truths which have had the effect of making the several parts of the brain independent; but this book is built on a logical structure of thought so that the other part of the brain is obliged to be continually active and to be brought into play as it were. It is the peculiar characteristic of a movement resting on an occult basis not only to pay attention to what in the abstract sense is right and to impart it as one thinks best; but it is necessary to impart it in a healthy way and, as honestly as possible, see to it that these matters are not given out for the sake of popularity in such a way that they may do harm. In Anthroposophy it is not simply a question of imparting the appropriate truths in books and lectures; it is a question of *how* they are written and communicated. And it is all the better if those who wish to be the vehicle of such a movement refuse to allow themselves to be deterred from imparting this or that for the sake of popularity. In Anthroposophy, more than in any other domain, it is important to adhere to the plain, unvarnished truth. And when one touches upon such questions as the transformation of the human sheaths through the practice of Anthroposophy, one realises immediately how necessary it is to present Anthroposophy to the world in the right way.

I should like to point out that the lectures which I propose to give must be taken as a whole and that certain doubts that might arise in the minds of some of the audience on hearing this first lecture will be dispelled later.

LECTURE TWO

The Hague, 21 March 1913

To the anthroposophist the effects of esotericism or Anthroposophy upon the etheric and astral bodies and the Ego are far more intimate than upon the physical body. Nevertheless, we shall lay a firm foundation for the next lectures, in which we have to consider the more spiritual members of the human make-up from this point of view, if we also bear in mind what can be said about the modifications of the physical sheaths. But it must be emphasised that the modifications indicated here do not refer to the highest stages of initiation, but rather to the earlier stages of the esoteric or anthroposophical life, and therefore are of general importance.

You will have gathered from yesterday's lecture that, through the influences I have described, the physical body of man becomes so to speak more vitally alive, inwardly more mobile, and on that account it may become difficult to endure. We feel its presence more than we normally do in everyday life, in ordinary life. We shall have to speak later of the difference between vegetable and animal food in connection with the other sheaths, but this difference plays an enormous part in the structure and organisation of the physical body. It must be emphasised of course that we have no wish to advocate a particular kind of diet, but only to state the facts in this domain. And as the soul develops, the facts in question become a matter of personal experience.

We know from experience that when we eat meat greater demands are made upon our physical body; it bears a heavier burden than when we live on a vegetarian diet. I pointed out yesterday that the physical body in the course of development contracts or shrinks, as it were, detaches itself from the higher spiritual members. Now when flesh foods are consumed, they are felt, as described in the last lecture, as a foreign substance which is integrated into the human organism, or, to use a more radical expression, as a thorn in the flesh. In esoteric development we feel so to speak the terrestrial weight of animal food more than we normally do and especially we experience the fact that flesh foods stimulate the instinctive life of the will. The life of the will, which for the most part is unconscious and which is active more in the emotions and passions, is stimulated by flesh foods. The observation that warlike peoples have a greater tendency to consume flesh foods than pacific peoples is therefore perfectly correct. But this need not lead to the erroneous belief that vegetable food must (of necessity) deprive man of all courage and energy. Indeed we shall see that what a person loses in the matter of instincts, of aggressive passions and emotions through abstention from flesh foods – we will discuss this later when we come to speak of the astral body – all this finds an inner compensation in the life of the soul. All these things are connected with the whole relationship of man and the other kingdoms of nature to the cosmos and we gradually receive – though not yet through higher clairvoyance – a kind of proof or confirmation of what the occultist affirms concerning the relationship between human life and the cosmos. We receive a sort of proof when, through this experience of the processes of the physical body which have become more active and mobile, we come to know, to a certain extent, in our own body the nature and properties of the natural products of the earth used as foodstuffs.

It is interesting to compare three kinds of food in relation to their cosmic significance – first, milk and milk products, secondly the plants and the foods that are prepared from them, and finally flesh foods. We can compare milk, plants and animal flesh as foods when, through esoteric development, we have become more sensible of their effects in ourselves. It will then be easier for us to confirm the statements arising from a rational observation of the external world. From occult observation of the cosmos you would find milk substance on earth, but on no other planet of our solar system. What is produced in a similar manner within the organism of living beings on other planets in our solar system would be something totally different from terrestrial milk. Milk is specifically of the earth. If we wanted to generalise about milk we should have to say that the beings inhabiting each planetary system have their own particular milk. If we examine the plant system of our earth and compare it occultly with the plant systems of other planets, with what corresponds to it on other planets, we must say that the forms of the plants on our earth are different from those on other planets of our solar system, but the inner being of the plants on earth is not merely terrestrial, but belongs to the solar system, that is, that the plant-nature of our earth is related to that of the other planets of our solar system. Thus there is a solar element in our plants that can also be found on other planets of our solar system. As for the animal kingdom, it follows from what has been said about milk that the animal kingdom on earth – and this can easily be demonstrated occultly – is radically different from any corresponding kingdom on other planets. Let us consider the action of milk food on the human body – for the moment we will limit ourselves to man. To the occultist milk signifies that which binds him to the earth as it were, to our planet; as a member of the common species of mankind it links him with the human race on earth. That mankind, in relation to the physical system of sheaths, also constitutes a whole is due to the fact that milk as a living food provides sustenance for living beings of animal provenance. Everything that milk supplies to the human organism prepares man for life on earth, unites him with terrestrial conditions, but does not actually chain him to the earth. It makes him a citizen of the earth, but does not prevent him at the same time from being a citizen of the whole solar system.

Flesh food has a different effect. Flesh food which is derived from the domain which is specifically terrestrial and which is not obtained, like milk, directly from the life processes of the living being, human or animal, but from that part of the animal substance which has already been transformed by the animal, this flesh food chains man especially to the earth. It makes him into a terrestrial creature and we must therefore say that insofar as he permeates his own organism with the effects of flesh food he deprives himself of the forces which liberate him from the earth. Through a meat diet he binds himself especially to the planet earth. Whilst milk enables him to be a citizen of the earth, as a temporary stage in his development, flesh food condemns him, unless he is raised to a higher stage by something else, to make his sojourn on earth a permanent sojourn to which he adapts himself completely. And the resolve to live on a milk diet signifies: I wish to remain on earth in order to be able to fulfil my task there, but not to dwell there permanently. The determination to live on a meat diet signifies: life on earth appeals to me to such an extent that I renounce the joys of heaven for I prefer to be wholly absorbed in the conditions of terrestrial existence.

Vegetarian diet is a diet that stimulates in the organism those forces which bring man into a kind of cosmic union with the whole of the planetary system. What man has to accomplish, when he continues to assimilate plant food in his organism, activates forces contained in the whole solar system, so that man in his physical sheath participates in these solar forces; he does not become alienated from them, he is not detached from them. This is something which the soul in the course of its anthroposophical or esoteric development gradually can experience in itself, namely, that with the intake of plant food it assimilates not something possessing terrestrial weight, but something pertaining to the sun, that is to say, to the central body of the entire planetary system. The lightness of the organism which results from a vegetarian diet lifts man above terrestrial heaviness and makes possible one might say a gradual responsiveness that develops into a certain inner perception of taste in his organism; it is as if this organism really shared with the plants the sunlight which contributes so much to the growth and flowering of plants.

From what has been said you will gather that in occult,

esoteric development it is extremely important not to chain oneself, as it were, to the earth, not to be weighed down with earth forces through the consumption of flesh foods if it can be avoided as far as individual and hereditary circumstances permit; the ultimate decision must depend upon the personal circumstances of the individual. It will be of real assistance to the whole development of man's life if he can dispense with a meat diet. On the other hand certain difficulties might arise if a person were to become a fanatical vegetarian in the sense of rejecting milk and all milk products. In this case the spiritual development of the soul may incur certain dangers because, in rejecting milk and milk products, a person may easily develop a love solely for that which detaches him from the earth and he may thus lose the threads uniting him with human activities on earth. It should be carefully noted that, in a certain sense, it is a good thing if the anthroposophical seeker, by his fanatical enthusiasm for the spiritual, does not create an obstacle in his physical body which would divorce him from all relationship to what is earthly and human. In order that we may not become fanatics of psychic development, in order that we may not be alienated from human feeling and human activities on earth, it is a good thing, as pilgrims on earth, to allow ourselves, to a certain extent, to take on "ballast" through consumption of milk and milk products. And it may even be a systematic training for the person who is not only able, so to speak, to live perpetually in the spiritual world and thereby becomes estranged from the earth, but who, in addition, has tasks to fulfil on earth, it may be a systematic training not to be a strict vegetarian, but to take milk and milk products as well. His organism, his physical body will thereby be related to the earth and mankind without chaining it to the earth, without burdening it with terrestrial existence as is the case with a flesh diet.

It is interesting therefore in every way to see how these things are connected with cosmic secrets, and how through the knowledge of these cosmic secrets one can follow the actual effect of nutritive substances in the human organism. As people who are interested in occult truths you must be increasingly aware that what exists on earth – and our physical body is an integral part of our terrestrial existence – depends not only on terrestrial conditions, but also on supra-mundane and cosmic forces and conditions. And this arises in a variety of ways. Let us take, for example, protein which is present in the hen's egg. We must clearly understand that this animal protein is not merely what the chemist finds in his analysis, but that, in its structure, it is the result of cosmic forces. Fundamentally these cosmic forces only work upon the protein after they have first acted upon the earth itself and above all upon the moon which accompanies the earth. The cosmic influences upon protein are therefore indirect; they first act upon the earth which, in its turn, reacts upon the composition of the protein with the forces it receives from the cosmos. It is the moon which plays the major part, but only because it first receives the forces from the cosmos and then, with the forces that it radiates, reacts upon the animal protein. In the smallest cell of the animal, and therefore in protein also, he who is endowed with clairvoyant vision can see that not only the terrestrial physical and chemical forces are present, but that the smallest cell of a hen's egg is built up of forces which the earth receives from the cosmos. The substance we call protein therefore is indirectly connected with the cosmos, but this animal protein substance as we know it on earth would never exist without earth conditions. It could not originate directly out of the cosmos; it is entirely a product of that which the earth must receive from the cosmos.

Again, what we know as the fatty substance of living beings which also forms part of human food, especially of those who eat meat, has a different effect. What we call fat, irrespective of whether a person eats it or whether the body itself manufactures it, is built up in accordance with entirely different cosmic laws from those which form protein. Whilst the cosmic forces of the Beings of the Spirits of Form are concerned with the latter, those Beings called Spirits of Movement are chiefly concerned with the production of the fatty substance. It is important to speak of these matters because it is only by discussing them in this way that one realises how complicated in reality is that which physical science imagines to be so infinitely simple. No living being could assimilate protein on the one hand, or fat on the other hand, without the cooperation from the cosmos, even though indirectly, of the Spirits of Form and the Spirits of Movement. Thus we can trace the spiritual effects of the activity of the different Hierarchies even into the substance of which our physical body consists. Therefore the experience that we have in relation to the protein and fat content of our physical body becomes in itself more differentiated, more mobile when the soul has undergone anthroposophical development. We are sensible of a twofold experience. That which in the normal life of man is merged into a single experience he now experiences as the separate action of the fats and proteins in the human organism. As the whole physical organism becomes more mobile the soul learns to distinguish two different experiences; one which so permeates us inwardly that we feel: to this I owe my physical organisation, my physical form . . . we are then aware of the proteins within us. And when we feel: this makes us indifferent to our inner isolation, this lifts us, as it were, above our physical body, this makes us more phlegmatic in relation to our inner feeling . . . when therefore a certain phlegma is added to our own experience (these experiences differ widely with anthroposophical development), then the origin of this latter experience is the presence of the fat in the physical body. Thus our inner experience in relation to the physical body becomes more complex.

We perceive this particularly in the case of starches or sugar. And in this respect sugar is very characteristic, for, from the point of view of taste, it is sharply differentiated from other substances. This differentiation can be clearly seen in ordinary life, not only in children, but also frequently in elderly people who have a sweet tooth. But usually this differentiation is restricted to the palate. When the soul undergoes development it experiences the intake of sugar and the sugar content of the body as something that gives it inner stability, inner support, and permeates it to a certain extent with a kind of natural egohood. In this respect one can extol the virtues of sugar. In fact, one who is developing spiritually often notices that he needs sugar because the aim of psychic development is to become progressively more selfless. Through a sound anthroposophical training the soul of itself becomes more selfless. Now in order that a man, who by virtue of his physical body has a terrestrial task to fulfil, may not lose the link of his Ego-organism with the earth, it is a good thing to create a counterpoise in the physical domain where egohood does not play so important a part as in the moral sphere. The consumption of sugar creates, as it were, a kind of innocent egohood which may form a counterpoise to the necessary selflessness in the moral and spiritual sphere. Otherwise man would all too easily be tempted to become not only selfless, but also to become a dreamer and visionary, to lose the capacity for sound judgement on mundane affairs. The addition of a certain quantity of sugar to the food, despite all man's aspiration to the spiritual world, helps to anchor him firmly to the earth, to cultivate in him a healthy perspective on terrestrial matters.

As you see, these things are complicated. But everything becomes complicated when one seeks to penetrate the real secrets of life. Thus, as the anthroposophist develops spiritually he sometimes feels that, in order not to be exposed to a false selflessness, to a loss of personality, he needs sometimes additional sugar. And then he can say: I am adding to myself something that, without lowering my moral tone, gives me, as if involuntarily, as if by a higher instinct, a certain stability, a certain egohood. On the whole one can say that the consumption of sugar enhances physically the individual characteristics of a person. We can be so certain of this that we can say that for those who have a sweet tooth – and this of course must be kept within healthy limits – it is easier to imprint their personal character on their physical body than for those who do not take sugar. These things may even lead to an understanding of something that can also be observed externally. In countries where, according to statistics, sugar consumption is low, the inhabitants have a less defined personality than in countries where consumption is high. If you visit countries where the people show more individuality, where each individual is self-contained, and then move on to countries where the inhabitants betray more the typical racial characteristics, show less individuality in their outward appearance, you will find that in the former countries sugar consumption is high, in the latter very low.

If we wish to have further examples of the effects of foods, let us consider the effects of certain stimulants, especially of coffee and tea. The effect of the consumption of coffee or tea upon the ordinary person is intensified in the case of the anthroposophist. As I have said, this is not a polemic for or against coffee, but simply a statement of things as they are, and I beg you to accept it only in this sense. In the normal life of man coffee and tea act as stimulants, but the stimulating effect of the consumption of coffee and tea upon the emotions is felt more keenly by the soul that is undergoing spiritual development. The action of coffee, for example, upon the human organism is to lift the etheric body out of the physical body, but in such a way that the physical body is felt as a solid foundation for the etheric body. Such is the specific effect of coffee. When coffee is taken, these two bodies are felt to be differentiated, but in such a way that the physical body, especially in its formal characteristics, is felt, under the influence of coffee, to radiate into the etheric body, as a kind of solid foundation for what is experienced through the etheric body. This must not be taken as a defence of coffee-drinking, for all this takes place upon the physical plane. A person would become a completely dependent being if he wanted to prepare himself spiritually by the use of these stimulants. We are only concerned with characterising the influence of these stimulants. But because logical, consistent thinking depends especially upon the structure and form of the physical body, the peculiar action of coffee throws into sharp relief the physical structure and promotes physically logical consistency. Consumption of coffee furthers by physical means logical consistency, consistent thinking based on facts. And though it may be injurious to health to drink large quantities of coffee, for those who wish to rise to spiritual heights it is not particularly harmful. It may be a good thing occasionally to have recourse to the stimulation of coffee in order to promote logical consistency. One might say that it seems quite natural for the person whose profession is writing and who does not quite find the logical sequence from one sentence to the next and who therefore chews his pencil in search of inspiration to turn to coffee for stimulation. This seems quite comprehensible to one who understands how to penetrate to the secret occult foundation of these things. Though as citizens of the earth we sometimes need this drink according to individual circumstances, it must be emphasised that coffee, despite its dangers to health, can contribute in a large measure towards the reinforcement of stability. Not that it should be recommended as a means to this end; but it has this capacity to promote stability and if, for example, the neophyte is inclined to let his thoughts stray in the wrong direction, we need not take it amiss if he makes himself more stable by drinking coffee.

It is different in the case of tea. Tea produces an analogous effect, a kind of differentiation between the physical nature and the etheric nature; but seen clairvoyantly the structure of the physical body in this case is in a certain sense less clearly defined whilst the tendency of the etheric body to fluctuate is emphasised. As a result of drinking tea thoughts become dissociated, unstable, less capable of adhering to facts. Tea, it is true, stimulates imagination, but not always in a very desirable sense; it does not make for fidelity to truth, or for accommodation to the reality of circumstances. It is comprehensible therefore that in social gatherings where great store is set upon flashes of wit, intellectual virtuosity, the stimulation is readily provided by tea. On the other hand it is also comprehensible that when the habit of tea-drinking is excessive it engenders a certain indifference to the demands that the healthy structure of his physical, earthly body may make upon man. So dreamy fantasy and a certain nonchalant insouciance that ignores the solid demands of practical life are easily encouraged by tea-drinking. And the soul undergoing spiritual development does not favour tea because tea-drinking leads more easily to charlatancy than coffee-drinking. The latter makes for greater stability, the former for greater charlatanism, although these descriptions are far too radical. All these are things which, as we have said, can be experienced thanks to the mobility which an anthroposophical training brings to the physical sheath of man.

I would simply like to add – and you can meditate further on these things or try to experience them personally – that if coffee-drinking promotes something like stability in the physical sheath and tea-drinking favours charlatanism, then chocolate mainly promotes philistinism. Chocolate is the true beverage of the bourgeoisie; it can be felt by direct experience when the physical body becomes more mobile. Chocolate can be recommended for bourgeois festivities and it is very understandable – excuse this parenthesis – that at family festivals, christenings, birthday celebrations, especially in certain circles on festive occasions, chocolate is the customary beverage. When we bear in mind that these beverages are stimulants, their influence assumes a greater significance, because what we normally experience in relation to foodstuffs influences our ordinary daily life in such a way that not only are we aware of the fundamental substance of which the body is constructed and which is constantly renewed, but we are also made aware, as was mentioned yesterday, of the inner independence, of the dissociation of the organs from one another. That is important and very significant.

And here we must emphasise especially that the relationship between the physical body and the physical heart becomes comprehensible to occult observation. The physical heart of man is to the occultist an extremely interesting and important organ; it can only be understood if we bear in mind the whole reciprocal relationship, including the spiritual relationship, between the sun and the earth. When, after the Sun epoch, the Old Sun was a kind of planetary precursor of the earth, at that moment there began the preparation, so to speak, of the relation which now exists between these two celestial bodies, the sun and the earth. And we must bear in mind this relation between the sun and the earth because we thereby fully understand how the earth of today is first nourished by solar activities which it assimilates and transmutes. What the solid substance of the earth absorbs in the form of solar forces, what the earth absorbs in its sheaths of air and water, in its changing conditions of warmth, what it absorbs in the light irradiating the earth, what it absorbs in that part of the earth (now no longer physically perceptible) which participates in the harmony of the spheres, the life forces it receives directly from the sun – all this is related to the inner forces which act upon the human heart through the circulation of the blood. In reality all these forces act upon the circulation of the blood and through the blood upon the heart. Modern theories on this question are completely wrong; according to modern scientific theory the heart acts as a pump that pumps the blood through the body and so the heart is regarded as the organ which regulates the circulation of the blood. But the exact opposite is true. The circulation of the blood is primary; and through its rhythmic pulsations, systole and diastole, the heart responds to what takes place in the circulation of the blood. It is the blood that drives the heart and not the heart that drives the blood. And the whole of this organisation which is concentrated in the activity of the heart is none other than the human microcosmic reflection of those macrocosmic activities that the earth first receives from the sun. What the earth receives from the sun is reflected in the relationship between the blood and the heart.

With the brain, however, the position is different. I mentioned yesterday some of the correspondencies of the brain. The human brain has little to do directly with the solar activities on the earth. Directly, I say; but indirectly, as an organ of perception, it is very much concerned with them in that it perceives, for example, the external light and colours; but that is perception. But directly, in its structure, in its inner mobility, in its whole inner life, the brain has little, in fact virtually nothing to do with the activities of the sun upon the earth; it is more concerned with all that rays down upon the earth from beyond our solar system. It is concerned with the cosmic conditions of the whole starry heavens, but not with the more limited conditions of our solar system. What we call the cerebral substance is more closely related to the moon, but only in so far as the moon is not dependent upon the sun, has preserved its independence of the sun. So that which takes place in our brain corresponds to activities lying outside the forces which find their microcosmic human reflection in our heart. Sun dwells in the human heart; what is present in the cosmos beyond the sun dwells in the human brain.

In relation to these two organs man is therefore a microcosm; through his heart he is exposed to the influences exercised by the sun upon the earth and reflects these influences, as it were. But through the brain he enjoys an inner life that is directly connected with the cosmos beyond the sun. This is an extremely important and significant relationship. The brain is connected with what the sun effects on the earth only through external perception; it is precisely in anthroposophical development that this is overcome; anthroposophical development triumphs over the world of the senses. Thus the brain is set free to develop an inner life that is so cosmic that even the sun is something far too specialised for its influence to be effective there. When the seeker surrenders himself in meditation to Imaginations of some kind, then processes take place in the brain which are unrelated to our solar system, but which correspond to the processes outside our solar system. Thus a certain relationship is established between the heart and the brain, akin to that existing between the sun and the starry heavens; and in a certain respect this is manifested in the experience of the developing soul, because whilst this soul is given over in earnest meditation to purely anthroposophical thoughts, the heart forms a kind of counter-pole, sets up a kind of opposition one might say to the stellar brain. This opposition is expressed in the fact that the neophyte learns to feel that the heart and brain begin to follow divergent paths; whilst hitherto he had had no need to direct his attention to each of them separately, but only to the manner in which they acted in conjunction, he must now begin to pay attention to them separately as he develops spiritually.

We have a remarkable conception of man's place in the cosmos when we consider the physical sheath of man in this way and bear in mind his position on earth. Through his blood system and heart he reflects the whole relationship between the sun and the earth and when inwardly he surrenders entirely to those things for which on earth he needs his physical brain as instrument, then there are present in the brain cosmic processes operating from beyond our solar system. We shall then realise that the neophyte has an entirely new experience with regard to his heart and brain. His impressions are clearly differentiated, so that he learns to feel on the one hand the processes of his brain in the silent course of the stars at night and on the other hand he feels the movements of the solar system in his heart. And thus you see at the same time a path which at a higher degree of initiation becomes a more important path, for this is the path leading from man to the cosmos! He who, through higher development, as described even in the exoteric lectures, stands outside his body, looks back upon it and fully understands all its processes, comes to recognise, in fact, in the circulation of the blood and the activity of the heart a reflection of the hidden forces of the solar system, and in the processes of his brain which he then sees spiritually from without, the secrets of the cosmos.

The observation expressed in the last sentence is connected with a comment I once made in Copenhagen and which found its way into my book *The Spiritual Guidance of Man*. You will gather from this that, in a certain respect, even the structure of the brain is a sort of reflection of the position of the heavenly bodies at the time of a man's birth in that geographical region where he is born. It is sometimes useful to return to these questions from another point of view because you will then have an idea of the scope of occult science and of the narrow-mindedness of certain critics when such an observation is made from this or that point of view. Of course it may appear arbitrary to explain important facts, such as this reflection of the stellar world in the human brain, from a certain point of view. But when supported by other points of view it will be found that they agree mutually. You will become aware of many more streams of occult science which converge and their confluence will provide increasingly a solid proof, even a rational proof, of things which if expressed from a single point of view might sometimes appear daring. From this you can perceive the delicacy and economy of the whole human structure. And if you now reflect that man takes in nourishment and by virtue of this binds himself to the earth, and only liberates himself again through certain substances – especially a vegetarian diet – if you reflect that precisely through assimilation of food man must make himself a citizen of the earth, you will then understand the tripartite division of man in relation to his physical sheath. Through his brain man belongs to the whole stellar universe; through his heart and everything connected with it he belongs to the sun; through his digestive system and everything associated with it he is, in another sense, a terrestrial being.

This also may be experienced and is experienced when the external physical sheath of man becomes in itself more mobile. Through what he absorbs from the earth alone a man may grievously sin against the pure forces of the cosmos which are manifested in him. By provoking disturbances through his choice of physical food, for example, he may trespass against the purely terrestrial laws governing digestion and which also work as solar laws in the activity of the heart and in the form of cosmic laws outside the solar system in the activity of the brain – man, through his food, may grievously sin against the cosmic activities in his brain; and this can be experienced by the soul in the course of spiritual development, particularly at the moment of awakening. During sleep the digestive activity extends to the brain, penetrates into the brain. On waking the intellectual activity penetrates to the brain and the assimilative activity of the brain declines. When thinking remains dormant during sleep, the digestive activity works into the brain and when a person wakes up and notices an after-effect of this, this experience may well be a true barometer of the wholesome or unwholesome nature of his food. Man feels, as it were, the introduction of an organic activity into his brain as deadening, stabbing sensations which may sometimes appear, if he has eaten something unsuitable, as little centres of insensibility in the brain. All this is experienced in the most delicate manner by the developing soul. And the moment of awakening is tremendously important for the perception of the conditions of health in the physical sheath which depend upon the digestion. Through perceptions which become progressively more delicate and are localized in the head, the neophyte perceives whether he violates in his nutrition the cosmic laws outside our solar system or whether he is in harmony with them. Here you see the wonderful relationship between the physical sheath and the whole cosmos, and the moment of awakening as a barometer indicating whether, through his digestion, he is violating cosmic conditions or is acting in harmony with them.

These observations will gradually prepare us for the transformations which take place in the etheric or astral body of man through esoteric or anthroposophical development.

LECTURE THREE

The Hague, 22 March 1913

After discussing man's physical system of sheaths we now come to the etheric system, to the etheric body. Here the modifications that take place in man through occult or anthroposophical development are concerned with the muscular system and especially with the senses, the sense organs. Man not only feels his muscular system becoming gradually more mobile – and the same could be said in respect of the other physical organs – but, in addition, he feels that this muscular system, apart from the fact that it is more vitally alive, is still permeated, as it were, by a dim consciousness. It is as if consciousness extended to the whole muscular system. And if we were to speak somewhat paradoxically, though not inaccurately, about this experience we might say that in the course of esoteric development we gradually become inwardly aware of the individual muscles and muscular system in a dream-like way; we are dimly aware at times of the activity of the muscular system during waking consciousness. It is nevertheless very interesting to consider this modification of the physical sheath because our perception of this phenomenon provides the best confirmation that in a certain direction we have made some progress. When we begin to sense our several muscles so that when, for example, we tense or relax them, we have a dim consciousness of what is taking place, a dim feeling of sympathy, then we must say that something is taking place in the muscles. When we are dimly aware of the movements of our muscles this is a proof that we are gradually beginning to feel the etheric body which impregnates the physical body: for what we actually feel are the forces of the etheric body which are active in the muscles. It is the first stage in the perception of the etheric body when we have a dim consciousness of our several muscles, a dream-like consciousness of our muscular system, as it were, just as we find in anatomical text-books a representation of man where the skin has been removed to expose the underlying muscles. Indeed when we begin to perceive the etheric entity we experience something akin to this stripping off of the skin and exposure of the muscles, a dim consciousness of our several members as of a kind of marionette, a jointed doll.

Less agreeable is man's susceptibility, a susceptibility which he never overcomes, when the bony-system first begins to dawn on his consciousness. It is less welcome because, when he becomes aware of the skeleton, he is brought face to face with the fact that he is gradually ageing. Therefore it is not very pleasant to call attention to this vulnerability in respect of the skeleton, a vulnerability which is not usually felt in normal life; but when man develops etherically he begins to feel the bony-system as a shadowy form within him. And he then understands that the symbolical representation of death as a skeleton was in accordance with an ancient clairvoyant faculty of mankind. They knew that man gradually feels the approach of death in his skeleton.

Far more important than all this is the experience we have of our sense-organs in the course of esoteric development. We know that the sense-organs must be eliminated when the neophyte undergoes esoteric development; they must be silent so to speak. During esoteric development the sense-organs feel therefore that they are condemned to inactivity. But because they are shut off, something else takes their place. We gradually become aware of the individual sense-organs as separate worlds which penetrate us. We begin to feel as if the eyes, the ears, even the sense of warmth has been "bored" into us. But what we begin to feel are not the physical sense-organs, but the etheric forces, the forces of the etheric body which fashion the sense-organs. So that when we shut off the activity of the sense, we see the nature of these sense-organs appearing as so many etheric organisations implanted into us. This is extremely interesting.

LECTURE THREE

To the extent that during esoteric development we eliminate the eye, for example, and are no longer concerned with physical sight, to that extent we learn to recognise that light organisms penetrate our organism. We then know that the eye has gradually been fashioned by the activity of the inner forces of light upon our organism. Whilst we suppress all activity of the physical eye we feel the visual field to be permeated by the etheric forces of light which fashion the eye. That we come to know the forces of light by eliminating vision is indeed a strange phenomenon. All the theories of physics are as nothing compared to the knowledge of the inner nature of light and its effects which we experience when, having disciplined ourselves to extinguish the physical vision of the eye, we are gradually able to perceive in its place the inner nature of the etheric forces of light.

The sense of warmth is at a lower stage, as it were. It is extremely difficult to eliminate sensitivity to heat and cold. During the period of meditation our best answer to this problem is to aim at an even temperature in the room, neither too hot nor too cold, so that we feel no sense of discomfort. If we are successful in this we can gradually learn to recognise the inner nature of the warmth-ether radiating through space – but it is difficult to distinguish this from the ordinary perception of temperature. Only then do we feel that our body is permeated by the activity of the warmth-ether. When we no longer have a perception of warmth itself, then we come to know the nature of the warmth-ether through personal experience.

The sense of taste is of course eliminated during esoteric exercises, but if we succeed in recalling the sensation of taste, we have a means of recognising the nature of an ether still finer than the light ether – the so called chemical ether. This is not very easy, but it is possible for us to experience it. In the same way, by shutting off the sense of smell, we can experience the life ether.

The suppression of hearing provides a strange experience. In this case we must attain such a capacity for detachment that we no longer hear audible sounds in our immediate environment. Everything audible must be excluded. Then, as though "bored" into the organism, the forces of the etheric body that fashioned our organ of hearing manifest themselves. We thus make an astonishing discovery. These matters belong, in fact, to ever higher mysteries. We have no hesitation in saying that one cannot grasp immediately all that is said with regard to these experiences in relation to such a sense as that of hearing. We discover that the human ear with its wonderful organisation could not possibly have been formed by the etheric forces which play round the earth. These light forces, these etheric forces of light, are intimately connected with the formation of our eyes, although the design for the eyes was already in existence earlier; but the structure of the eye and its position in the organism is closely related to the forces of the light ether of the earth. In the same way our sense of taste is connected with the forces of the chemical ether of the earth and to a large extent is developed out of them. Our sense of smell is related to the life ether and is almost entirely formed from the life ether of the earth. But when our organ of hearing is experienced occultly during esoteric development, it reveals that it owes only an infinitesimal part of its existence to the etheric forces of the earth. It might be said that the terrestrial forces have put the finishing touch on our organ of hearing, but their influence upon this organ has been such that they have made it not in effect more perfect, but more imperfect, for these etheric forces can only act upon the ear because they are active in the air and the air continually offers resistance to them.

Hence we may say, although it seems paradoxical, that our organ of hearing is the degenerate offshoot of a much finer organisation which formerly existed. And at this stage of development, through his own experience, the anthroposophist will realise that he brought with him the ear, the complete organ of hearing, when he made his way from the ancient Moon to the earth; he will find that this organ of hearing was far more perfect on the ancient Moon than it is upon the earth. In relation to the ear we gradually begin to feel a certain melancholy – we are obliged sometimes to make use of paradoxical expressions – because the ear belongs to those organs which in their disposition, in their entire structure, bear witness to past perfections. And he who gradually undergoes experiences briefly indicated here will understand the occultist who assuredly derives his knowledge from far deeper forces, the occultist who says to him that on the ancient Moon the ear had much greater significance for man than it has today. At that time the function of the ear was, so to speak, to live wholly in the music of the spheres which still resounded on the ancient Moon. And the ear was related in such a way to the sounds of the music of the spheres still resounding on the Moon, though more feebly now than in earlier times, that it responded to them. Thanks to its former perfection the ear was always steeped in music on the ancient Moon and this music was still communicated on the ancient Moon to the whole human organisation; the waves of music still permeated the human organisation, and the inner life of man consisted in a participation in the music around him, in an adaptation to this musical environment. The ear was the organ of communication; its purpose was to reproduce inwardly those movements which resounded externally as music of the spheres. On the ancient Moon man still felt himself to be a kind of instrument on which the forces of the cosmos played, and the ears, in their perfection, mediated at that time between the "artists" of the cosmos and the instrument of the human organism. Thus the present disposition of the organ of hearing serves to awaken a memory, and with this memory is associated the idea that, through a kind of degeneration of this organ, man has become incapable of hearing the music of the spheres; that he has emancipated himself therefrom and could only recapture this music of the spheres in the music of the present day which, in reality, can only be heard in the element of the air surrounding the earth.

We can also have experiences in relation to other senses, but, of course, they become ever more indefinite and there would not be much point in pursuing these experiences connected with other sense organs for the simple reason that it is difficult by means of ordinary human concepts to throw light on these modifications which are the fruit of esoteric development. What would be the use, for example, in relation to what man can now experience on earth, if one were to speak of the sense for speech. I do not mean the sense for the meaning of words. Those who heard my lectures on Anthroposophy in Berlin[1] already know that there is a special sense for speech. Just as there is a tonal sense, so there is a special sense which only has an inner organ, not an external one for the understanding of the spoken word itself. This sense has deteriorated still further so that today there only remains a last echo of what it once was on the ancient Moon. That which today has become the sense for speech, a means of communication, enabled man on the ancient Moon to feel his way consciously into the whole environment with imaginative consciousness in order, as it were, to find his way round the ancient Moon. What movements one made, the path one had to follow was determined by the sense for speech on the ancient Moon. One gradually learns to know this sense for the spoken word when one gradually develops a feeling for the inner value of vowels and consonants in mantric sentences. But what terrestrial man can achieve in general in this domain is but a faint echo compared with the speech sense in former times.

Thus you see how man gradually develops the perception of his etheric body, how that which he rejects in his occult development, namely, the activity of his physical senses, finds compensation on the other hand, in that it leads him to the perception of the etheric body. But strangely enough, when we experience these perceptions of the etheric body of which we have just spoken, we feel them as if they did not really belong to us, as if they had been implanted into us from outside. We feel as if the body of light had been "drilled" into us, as if something akin to a musical wave inaudible on earth had been "bored" into us through the ear; we do not feel the warmth-ether as bored into us, but as permeating us, and in place of the sense for taste which has been eliminated we begin to feel the activity of the chemical ether working in us, and so on. At this point, compared with what is called the normal condition, man feels his etheric body transformed, as if something had penetrated into it from outside.

LECTURE THREE

We now begin gradually to perceive our etheric body more directly. The most striking transformation that occurs in the etheric body, which, for many is most unwelcome and which is not recognised as a transformation, although it clearly is so, is that esoteric development clearly shows that at first the power of memory gradually declines. Through esoteric development ordinary memory must always suffer diminution. At first memory becomes weaker and he who wishes to avoid this should not undertake esoteric development. It is especially noticeable that the memory which may be described as the mechanical memory, the memory which is strongest in childhood and youth and which is generally implied when we speak of memory, ceases to be active and vigorous. And many esotericists have reason to complain of a decline in memory. And this decline soon becomes evident long before we are aware in ourselves of the delicate truths which have just been discussed. But just as our physical body – in spite of its becoming more mobile – can suffer no harm if we pursue the correct anthroposophical training, neither will the memory suffer any serious or lasting injury. We must simply endeavour to follow the right course.

As regards the physical organisation, whilst the body becomes more flexible externally, whilst inwardly its organs become more independent so that it is more difficult to reconcile them than before, we must develop inner strength. This is done by practising the six exercises described in the second part of my book *Occult Science – an Outline*. The neophyte who practises them in the manner prescribed will find that he gains as much in inner strength in order to keep the more mobile physical body under control as he loses in physical energy through esoteric development. In relation to the memory we must also follow the right course. We lose the memory that serves the purposes of the external life; but we need suffer no harm if we take care to develop greater interest, deeper interest in all that concerns us in life, a greater readiness to participate more than has been our wont hitherto. We must begin by developing a sympathetic interest in things which are of importance to us. Previously we developed a more mechanical memory which sometimes proves to be quite reliable in the case of things we wish to retain but for which we have no particular liking; but this mechanical memory ceases in time. We notice when undergoing an anthroposophical or esoteric development we easily forget things. The things for which we have no feeling, no love or sympathy, no psychic affinity are soon forgotten; on the other hand those for which we have affinity are retained all the better. We must therefore endeavour to develop systematically this psychic affinity. It is possible to have the following experience. Let us take the case of a person who in his youth before he became interested in anthroposophy had read a novel he was quite unable to forget; he could always recount the story again and again. Later, having studied anthroposophy he reads another novel; immediately he forgets the contents, he is unable to recount them. But if he takes up a book that he believes or is told is important to him, if he reads it through once and then tries immediately afterwards to repeat it mentally, and not only to repeat it, but to repeat it backwards, from the end to the beginning – if he takes the trouble to refer a second time to certain details, if he becomes so absorbed in it, if furthermore he takes a piece of paper and notes down a few thoughts on the subject and tries to ask himself the question: from what point of view are you particularly interested in this subject, then he will find that in this way he develops a different kind of memory. It is no longer the same memory. When we make use of it we are clearly aware of the difference. When we make use of the mechanical memory things arise in our soul as memories; but if, in the manner already described, we systematically cultivate our memory as anthroposophists, then the things we have experienced in this way appear as if they had remained stationary in time. We learn to look back into time, as it were, and it really seems as if we are looking back at the things we were recalling; indeed, we shall notice that things progressively assume a pictorial form, that the memory becomes increasingly more imaginative. If we have carried out what I have just described – with a book, for example – then, when it is necessary to recall the matter we need only touch upon something which is connected with it in some way and we shall then see the moment when we were busy reading the book. We shall see ourselves reading it. It is not the memory which is revived, but the whole picture arises in our consciousness. We shall then be able to perceive that, whilst previously we only read the book, now the contents actually appear. We see them as if at a distance in time; the memory becomes a seeing, or a perception of pictures at a distance in time.

This is the very first beginning, certainly a very elementary beginning of gradually learning to read the Akashic Record. Memory is replaced by learning to read the past. And very often a person who has undergone a certain esoteric development may have lost his memory almost completely; but he is none the worse for it for he sees things in retrospect. In so far as he himself was associated with them, he sees them with particular clarity. What I am now saying would be ridiculed by anyone who was not an anthroposophist because he has no idea of what it means when an esotericist assures him that he no longer has any memory, that he has lost his memory, and yet he knows perfectly well what has happened because he can see it in the past. Whereupon the former replies: "But you have an excellent memory!" He has no idea of the transformation that has taken place; it is a transformation of the etheric body that accounts for this.

Clearly then, this transformation of the memory is associated with something else; it is associated with the fact that we develop, so to speak, a new kind of comprehension of our inner being. We cannot develop this retrospective vision without at the same time adopting a certain attitude towards our past experience. Thus, when at a later date a man looks back on something he has done – as in the case of the book described above – when he sees himself in that situation, he will of course have to judge for himself whether he was wise or foolish to act as he did. With this retrospective view another experience is of necessity closely connected, a kind of self-criticism. The neophyte cannot do otherwise than define his attitude towards his past. He will reproach himself about certain things, he will be delighted that he has been successful in others. In short, he cannot do otherwise than pass judgement on the past he thus sees in retrospect, so that he becomes in fact a sterner judge of himself, especially of his past life. He feels the etheric body stirring within him, the etheric body which from the perspective of after-death bears within it the whole of the past; he feels this etheric body as an encapsulation, as something that lives in him and determines his worth as a human being. Indeed such a transformation takes place in the etheric body that he often feels the need to make this retrospective survey, to review certain actions in order to learn in a quite natural manner to judge of his own worth as a human being. Whilst normally one lives without being aware of the etheric body, we now perceive it in the retrospective survey of our own life. Our personal life gradually becomes an object of concern when we undergo an esoteric development. We must face the fact that the esoteric life gives us food for thought and that we must take a closer look at our merits and demerits, our errors and imperfections.

But something deeper becomes perceptible, something that is connected with the etheric body, something that could also be perceived formerly but not so decisively, that is the temperament. In the serious student of occultism a greater sensitivity in relation to his own temperament depends upon the transformation of his etheric body. Let us take a particular case which clearly illustrates this – the person of melancholic temperament. The melancholic who has not undergone esoteric development or studied Anthroposophy, who goes through life with a chip on his shoulder, who is easily moved to derogatory criticism and who reacts to things in such a way that they arouse his sympathy and antipathy more strongly than they would in the case of the phlegmatic type for example – such a melancholic with all his characteristics, from the extremes of contrariness, moroseness, hostility, contempt and hatred towards the world, to a great mellowness, a greater sensitivity towards the impressions of the world – for there are many shades between these two extremes – when this melancholic person undertakes an esoteric development, his temperament becomes fundamentally the instrument through which he can experience the etheric body. He becomes susceptible to the complex of forces which provoke his melancholy and which are clearly discernible in himself, and whilst formerly he simply directed his dissatisfaction against the external impressions of the world, he now begins to turn his dissatisfaction against himself.

In esoteric development it is very necessary that self-knowledge should be carefully practised; the neophyte should be advised to practise this self-knowledge which enables him as a melancholic to accept this transformation with calm and composure. Whilst formerly the world was often abhorrent to him he now turns this abhorrence against himself; he begins to criticise himself so that people see that all is not well with him. We can only judge these things correctly when we fully understand what is called temperament. A melancholic is only a melancholic because the melancholic temperament predominates in him; for fundamentally everyone is endowed with all four temperaments. Under certain circumstances a melancholic is also phlegmatic, under others he is sanguine and again under others, choleric; the melancholic temperament simply predominates over the other temperaments. And a phlegmatic person is not one who possesses only the phlegmatic temperament, but in whom the phlegmatic temperament is more pronounced, the other temperaments remain in the background.

Now just as the transformation of the etheric body in the confirmed melancholic leads him to turn his melancholy against himself, so modifications and new responses appear also in relation to the other temperaments. But, through wise self-knowledge, it is possible, in the course of esoteric development, to repair the damage done by the predominant temperament; one begins to feel convinced that this damage can be repaired by bringing about modifications with the other temperaments. Thus as a result of these modifications a balance is established between the temperaments. One must be aware of the effect of the transformations in relation to the other temperaments.

Let us suppose that a phlegmatic person becomes a student of esotericism; this would be no easy matter, but let us suppose that he develops into a really good esotericist. This is not impossible, because sometimes when a phlegmatic person receives powerful impressions, he is powerless against certain impressions, so that the phlegmatic temperament, when not too deeply infected with materialism, is often not a bad preparation for esoteric development; only it must appear in a nobler form than in the grotesque form, the sole form in which we are familiar with the phlegmatic temperament. When this phlegmatic person cultivates esotericism his phlegmatic temperament is transformed in a peculiar manner. He has then a strong inclination to observe himself very carefully, and that is why the phlegmatic temperament which is least troubled by careful self observation is not a bad preparation for an esoteric development, because it is entirely suited to calm self-observation. What he perceives in himself does not affect him as it affects the melancholic; his self-observations as a rule penetrate more deeply than those of the melancholic who is inhibited by the bouts of anger he directs against himself. The phlegmatic type whose soul develops is therefore the best material for serious anthroposophical development.

As I have already said, every man is endowed with the four temperaments and in the melancholic the melancholic temperament predominates. The phlegmatic temperament also exists in him. In the melancholic, one can always find aspects of his make-up where he acts as a phlegmatic under certain circumstances. When the melancholic becomes an esotericist and can be guided in some way – whilst on the one hand he will be certain to take himself to task and will continually reproach himself – we must endeavour to direct his attention to those things towards which he had previously been phlegmatic. His attention must be aroused in things which formerly did not appeal to him. If we are successful in this then the damage caused by his melancholy will be neutralised.

The person of sanguine temperament makes a strange esotericist. His chief characteristic is that he likes to hasten from one impression to another, and is unwilling to adhere to one impression. The modification of his etheric body brings a strange transformation; the moment he becomes interested or another seeks to interest him in esotericism he becomes phlegmatic or indifferent towards his own inner being, so that under certain circumstances the sanguine type, as regards his temperament, is the least promising material for esoteric development. When the sanguine person takes up esotericism or Anthroposophy, as he frequently does – for he is interested in all sorts of things including Anthroposophy and esotericism, though not very seriously and his interest may not last for long – he must acquire a kind of self-observation; but he accepts all this with great indifference; he does not care to look into himself. He is interested in this or that, but it does not go very deep. He discovers all sorts of interesting characteristics in himself but he is immediately satisfied with them; he likes to speak of a certain interesting characteristic, but the whole matter is soon forgotten, even what he observed in himself. And those who have only a temporary interest in esotericism and soon abandon it again are chiefly the sanguine natures.

Tomorrow we will endeavour to illustrate what I have been discussing today with the help of a diagram of the etheric body and we shall then show in addition the modification of the etheric body resulting from esoteric or anthroposophical development.

The situation is again different in the case of the choleric temperament. It is virtually impossible, or only possible on the rarest occasions to make the choleric into an esotericist. It is the hallmark of the choleric type, when the choleric temperament dominates his personality, to reject all esotericism out of hand; he does not wish to have anything to do with it. None the less it may happen that karmic conditions bring him to esotericism; it will then be difficult for him to modify his etheric body, for in the choleric this body is particularly dense and difficult to influence. In the melancholic, the etheric body is like an india rubber ball (forgive this trivial comparison, but it will illustrate my point) from which the air has been released; when one depresses it, the depression remains for some time. In the choleric person, the etheric body is like a fully inflated rubber ball; if one attempts to depress it, the depression is not maintained. The ball actively resists and reacts. Thus the etheric body of the choleric is not very elastic, it is tough and tenacious.

That is why he has great difficulty in modifying it; he cannot work upon himself. Therefore he rejects from the outset esoteric development which seeks to transform him; he cannot cope with himself, as it were. But if the choleric is faced with the vicissitudes of life, or if his temperament betrays a slight nuance of melancholy, then it is possible for him, through this nuance of melancholy, so to develop the choleric element in his organism that he struggles might and main against the resistance of his etheric body. And if he succeeds in modifying his etheric body, he develops within him a very special quality: through his esoteric development he becomes more capable than others of presenting objectively and profoundly the external facts in their causal and historical relationship. And he who can appreciate good historiography – good historical writing is rare amongst esotericists – a historiography that really allows the facts to speak for themselves, will nevertheless find here the beginning, the unconscious, instinctive beginning of that which the esotericist with a choleric temperament might achieve as historiographer, narrator or descriptive writer. Men like Tacitus, for example, were at the beginning of such an instinctive, esoteric development; hence his wonderful, incomparable descriptive power. An esotericist who reads Tacitus knows that this unique kind of historiography springs from a quite special elaboration of a choleric temperament in the etheric body. This is clearly manifested in writers who have undergone an esoteric development. Though not generally accepted, this applies equally to Homer. Homer owes his outstanding pictorial and descriptive power to the choleric temperament active in his etheric body. And in this domain many other factors could be cited which would prove, or at least substantiate in external life, the fact that when the choleric undergoes esoteric development he is specially qualified to portray the world in its reality, in its causal relationships. Thanks to his esoteric development therefore his descriptions, even in their external form, bear the stamp of truth and veracity.

Thus we see that the changes in the etheric body give expression quite particularly to human life that in this incarnation becomes more perceptible than before in the form it has hitherto possessed. The temperaments also become more perceptible in esoteric development, and for true self-knowledge it is particularly important to take the temperaments into account. We shall speak more about these things tomorrow.

LECTURE FOUR

The Hague, 23 March 1913

The more the etheric body of man is modified under the influence of esoteric development, the more he acquires what may be called a feeling for time. This feeling for time implies a feeling for the succession of facts and events in time. Normally, in external life, man lacks this definite feeling for time. Now I have already indicated briefly that this feeling for time arises through the transformation of the etheric body when, through esoteric development, we become more sensitive, for example, to the seasonal changes of summer and winter. But through the modification of the etheric body we experience the flux of events much more vividly, we are much more sensitive to it. And he who for some time has earnestly tried to develop his soul will perceive a distinct difference between the different seasons and even between certain parts of the seasons; he will gradually begin to feel inwardly a vast difference between summer and winter, between spring, summer and autumn, and also between shorter periods in the course of the year. Time in its progress becomes, so to speak, something living. We gradually become aware that in the course of time we perceive differentiated life. Just as in the physical body the individual organs are differentiated and become inwardly more alive and independent of one another, so the different periods of the continuous time-sequence become, to a certain extent, more independent of each other. And this is connected with the fact that with the development of our own etheric body we participate in the life of the external ether which surrounds us on all sides. We are surrounded not only by air, but also by the ether and this ether lives a real life in time.

LECTURE FOUR

The surrounding ether is in a certain sense a kind of living being; it lives, and lives differently according to the different moments of time, just as man lives differently according to his different ages. We learn to feel this continuity in the life of the external ether so that we increasingly acquire a feeling for the external life of the life ether when spring comes, when summer is approaching, when summer reaches its zenith and then declines, when autumn is approaching and when it has arrived. We learn to participate in this external process, to distinguish clearly between the life of summer-spring, summer-autumn, and that of real winter.

This difference becomes increasingly more perceptible so that ultimately we can say: the earth with its ether lives an independent life, and in so far as we live in time we are literally immersed in this changing of the ether. Midsummer is the time when we feel most clearly that, with our etheric body, we are, so to speak, thrown back upon ourselves and that with the earth we live a particular kind of life so that the earth then affects us inwardly very little. As we have already said we are thrown back upon ourselves and we gradually begin to understand what the occultist means when he says that summer is the time when the earth is asleep. We here touch upon a matter which, on account of the external *maya* that surrounds mankind, is quite falsely interpreted. In the external life dominated by *maya* we like to compare spring to the morning, summer to midday and autumn to evening. This comparison is false, for it bears no relation to reality. As a matter of fact, if we wish to compare the change of the seasons with something in ourselves, we must compare spring, summer and autumn, in this sequence, with the sleeping time of the earth, and autumn, winter and spring, in this order, with the waking time of the earth. And when we speak of the Spirit of the Earth, we must imagine that in the hemisphere where summer reigns the Spirit of the Earth during summertime is in the same condition, so to speak, that we are when we sleep. Of course it is different in the case of the earth. Man is either asleep or awake; in the case of the earth, one hemisphere is awake, whilst the other is asleep and vice versa.

Fundamentally the spirit of the Earth never sleeps; when, in the one hemisphere its waking activity is replaced by sleep, it then transfers its waking activity to the other hemisphere. But we can ignore this for the moment.

Let us rather consider man's participative experience in the life of the earth; we need only take into consideration a single hemisphere. We have to imagine that during summer the Spirit of the Earth separates in a certain way from its physical body, that is to say, from the earth itself, and that this Spirit of the Earth lives in summer in the same relationship to its physical body as man to his body during sleep.

During the period of sleep the physical body and the etheric body lie in the bed where they lead a purely vegetative life. To occult vision it appears that something unfolds in the body of the sleeping man like delicate vegetation, like a burgeoning of purely vegetal life, and the forces which have become exhausted during the waking life are restored by this vegetative life, so that for man his summer time is the period when he is asleep. And if he were to look down on his sleeping physical body, when with his astral body and his ego he is outside the physical body, he would see the physical body burgeoning like the plant life on earth in spring and summer. He would perceive in his physical body during sleep a burgeoning vegetative life of summer time.

But because the hemisphere of the earth that we inhabit has its sleeping time during summer, man, together with his etheric body is, to a certain extent, left to his own resources and the consequence is that thanks to esoteric development he is able – if he has developed the capacity – to perceive his etheric body better and more clearly in summer than in winter. He perceives, as it were, the independence of his etheric body and in our present epoch especially the independence of the etheric part of the head, the etheric part underlying the brain. It is a very strange experience when, through participating in the etheric life of the earth in summer one begins gradually to acquire a kind of inner feeling for this particular part of the human etheric body underlying the head. This inner experience is felt differently in spring, differently in summer and again differently

LECTURE FOUR

towards autumn. These differences of inner experience are so clearly felt that, just as we speak of a differentiation of the members of the physical body, so we may now speak of different lives we live through the course of summer, lives that are clearly distinguished from one another. The life that unfolds inwardly in spring is different from that which unfolds inwardly in summer, and that in autumn is again different. In speaking of the etheric body we must make the distinction that we shall make today – we shall clearly distinguish from the rest a particular etheric part underlying the head.

I will sketch this for you on the blackboard in a few strokes.* If we picture the human being in rough outline, we can imagine that this etheric body of which I have just spoken is perceived – indeed the upper part becomes less and less perceptible and is lost in indefiniteness – as floating with the stream of time. And we gradually begin to feel quite clearly that in this part of our etheric body Beings were working creatively, Beings who replaced one another, so to speak, in the seasonal changes – from spring to autumn. We perceive that the seasons have worked upon this cerebral part of our etheric body so that our etheric brain is in some respects a complex organ. It has been built up as it were, by different spiritual Beings who manifest their capacities in successive epochs. We now gain insight into a very important teaching that was cultivated especially in the schools of Zarathustra.[1] This teaching held that the etheric body of the human brain had been gradually created from out of the Cosmos by spiritual Beings called Amshaspands. And these Amshaspands exercised their sovereignty during summer, and indeed still hold sway today, replacing one another successively, the first ruling in early spring, the second in spring and so on up to the sixth and seventh. Seven, or rather six of these spiritual Beings work consecutively in time; they are the creative Spirits who – precisely because they work consecutively so that when one has completed his work the next takes over – create an entity as complex as the etheric body, especially the etheric body of the human brain. Six or seven spiritual Beings successively play into

* The relevant drawing was not preserved.

our brain. We shall only understand the physical brain of man when we can say: in the brain there acts a Spirit who can be felt especially in early spring – he sends forth his forces which at first are etheric forces; then in late spring comes a second Spirit, who in his turn sends forth his forces.

The etheric forces of this second Spirit therefore stream into the same space. The third Spirit in his turn pours in his etheric forces and thus is formed this etheric part of the human brain; Spirits who successively replace one another project their etheric forces into the same space.

Now we must clearly understand that we can only feel certain relationships in so far as our brain is related to these Spirits who today manifest their etheric forces outside us; for occultism teaches us that what I have just described took place during the ancient Moon period, so that we must not believe that these same Spirits who, as we may say, take command in summer are still active today as formative forces. Man has brought over with him into his earthly existence the aptitudes which were rayed in by these Spirits during the ancient Moon period; but because he bears them within his own etheric body, he can still feel today – when these spiritual Beings no longer have a direct influence on the inner etheric body of our brain – he can still feel the relationship with them and it is this which he feels in summer. In early spring we feel the first of these Spirits who today has another task externally in the ether; we feel that we owe to him what we bear within ourselves, what we received on the ancient Moon; we feel ourselves related to him at that time. During his esoteric development the neophyte can make the stupendous discovery that in the course of time he experiences within himself something like a reflection of active spiritual Beings who today have a quite different task than in the past when they cooperated in the creation of our being. During the formation of the earth the physical brain appeared as a reproduction, an imprint of what had developed as a kind of etheric prototype during the ancient Moon period, through these spiritual cosmic influences. I have depicted this part of our etheric body as open above because we feel it like this. (See diagram, p. 58.) And we feel it in this way because, as soon as we are aware of it in ourselves, we have the feeling: "You are opening yourself to the spiritual worlds; you are in touch with spiritual worlds that are always above you." There is a further impression that is gradually developed in esoteric life in relation to this part of the etheric body. . . . In general it is not easy to make oneself understood in these matters, but I hope that if I try to explain them clearly we shall be able to understand one another.

When we begin to feel our etheric body, it is as if we feel ourselves floating in the stream of time. But as regards the etheric part of the head we have the impression that, in a sense, we are taking time within us; not only do we feel that we are floating down the stream of time, but that we are part and parcel of the stream of time. In fact we carry a great deal belonging to an earlier age in this etheric part of the head, we carry the ancient Moon period here; for the most essential part of the head was developed at that time and in the etheric body of the brain we carry with us the stream of the ancient Moon period. And when we begin to feel this, it is like a memory of the time on the ancient Moon. He who forms an idea of the inner experiences which were described in the last lecture as experiences associated with the different temperaments can also understand the statement that the occultist who thus learns to feel the inner nature of the etheric body of the head, when he specially concentrates upon this etheric part of the head, always feels this concentration to be associated with a melancholy frame of mind which lays hold of him; in the course of his esoteric development he feels as if his head had been invaded by a mood of melancholy. And out of this mood there gradually dawns in his inner experience an understanding of the things imparted to our friends in the occult description of the ancient Moon.

Esoteric development must of course go much further if we really wish to describe the different conditions on the ancient Moon; but you see how things begin which lead to such a description. You see that there arises in man himself something that could be called the melancholy of the head and that within the frame of mind there gradually emerges a vision, like a memory vision into a far distant past into the ancient Moon period. From the descriptions which have just been given you would be well advised to ascertain how esoteric development proceeds; how starting from a particular experience one first learns to recognise this experience – in this case for example a memory of a remote past which we have carried with us on the stream of time into the present – and learns to unroll again, as it were, the scroll of that which has formerly been lived through. From this you will realise that the occultist is not indulging in idle fancies when he describes that structure of the universe which dates back to the ancient Moon, Sun and Saturn epochs, but that if we wait patiently and listen to the explanation of the manner in which these things have been arrived at, we can gain an idea of how it is possible gradually to live into those mighty and grandiose cosmic pictures which indeed belong to a far distant past but which can be called forth again from the life of the present. We must simply reach the stage of development when we experience within ourselves past events which lie concealed within us and bring them to the light of day.

The part of the etheric body which belongs to the central part of the human being is experienced in a different way. Externally, feeling is lost; inwardly it is perceived approximately in such a way that one can say: What is portrayed here [see diagram, p. 58] in the middle as a kind of ovoid form is felt to be detached from the rest. When we isolate this central part of the etheric body as a particular experience we must say: He who, through his esoteric development, manages to experience in himself the differentiated life of this central part of man also has the feeling that in this part of his etheric body he swims exactly with the stream of time. And in this part of his etheric body his participation in the etheric life of the earth which acquires a distinct and separate character according to the different seasons is still clearly felt.

He who progresses esoterically feels in this particular part of the etheric body that in early spring other Spirits are working upon him than those of midsummer or autumn. It is a kind of participation in, more precisely a kind of floating with, the stream of time. This part of the etheric body is thereby dissociated from the rest, and if we explore these matters more closely, the feeling we have in this central part of the etheric body alternates between the phlegmatic and sanguinic moods. This feeling assumes a wide variety of nuances between these two moods. In spring, for example, one feels as if the etheric body were floating with the stream of time – this is expressed differently in the physical body – and towards autumn it is rather a resistance to the stream of time, a withdrawal into oneself.

A third part of the etheric body, the lower part, is felt to lose itself in the indefinite, to vanish into the earth, but at the same time it becomes more widely diffused. These are the three parts of the etheric body which can be experienced separately.

Now this describes the *inner* feeling, the *inner* experience of the etheric body. To the clairvoyant, for example, this inner experience would be different if he were to observe the etheric body of another, for this is an inner experience of the etheric body. This experience is considerably modified by the existence of a fourth member of the etheric body, clearly delimited as a kind of ovoid form which embraces the whole man. From the different feelings experienced in relation to these parts of the etheric body we gradually have a feeling, an inner impression of the etheric body as of an external form.

Furthermore, the etheric body assumes different hues; the upper part appears to be enveloped in a kind of bluish or blue-violet (*blauviolett*) aura. This part which corresponds to the head is bluish or blue-violet according to the nature of the person and gradually passes over into a greenish colour (*grün*) below the head. The central part is distinctly yellow-red (*gelb-rötlich*) – assuming one sees the colour – and the lower part assumes a distinctly reddish (*rötlich*) to deep red colour which rays out and often covers a wide field.

Now the forces working in these four parts are differentiated, so that our inner feelings are not very definite; but when we look at this outermost aura clairvoyantly from without, the forces active in this aura compress the upper part and give the impression when seen from outside that the etheric part of the head is the same shape as the head, but a little larger. And the same applies to the central part. The further down one goes the less this applies. But because the forces work on each other, this gives the impression when seen from without that the etheric body is a kind of prototype of the physical body, but projects a

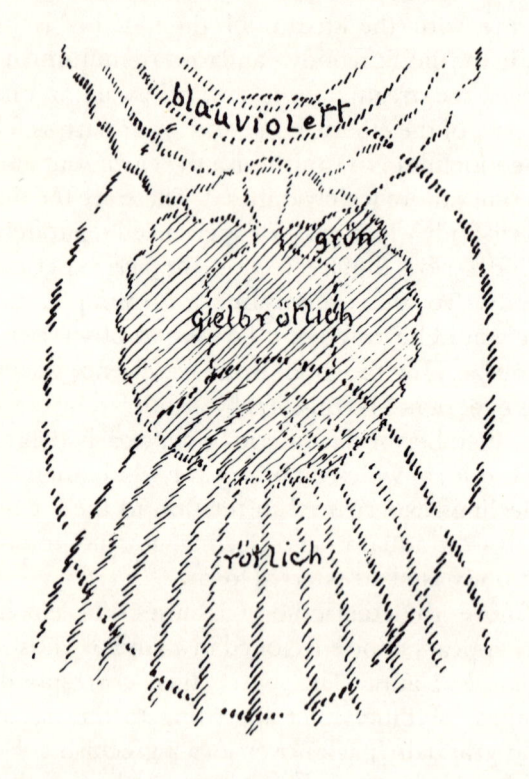

blauviolett

grün

gelbrötlich

rötlich

little beyond it. Towards the lower part, the feeling of the correspondence between the physical body and etheric body is gradually lost.

You must bear firmly in mind therefore that the inner experience of the etheric body is different from the being of the etheric body as revealed externally to clairvoyant vision. This must be clearly understood.

LECTURE FOUR

When through esoteric development you learn to pay attention to those fundamental temperaments latent in the etheric body which were described yesterday, you will find that in relation to the lower part of the etheric body the prevalent mood is choleric. Thus the various members of our etheric body are differentiated according to the different temperaments: the upper part is inclined to the melancholic temperament, the central part alternates between phlegmatic and sanguine, the lower part is inclined to the choleric. I beg you to note particularly that this description applies to the etheric body. He who fails to consider this carefully may easily fall into error if he takes these matters superficially. But he who takes this fully into account will be greatly struck by the agreement between what has been advanced here and certain phenomena of life. Let us look at a choleric person for a moment – he provides a very interesting study.

According to what has just been said, in the choleric person the lower part of the etheric body would be particularly pronounced and would predominate over the other parts – the typical characteristic of the choleric type. The other parts are also developed of course, but the lower part would be particularly predominant. Now when the lower part of the etheric body is especially developed as etheric body and is endowed with powerful forces, something else always occurs: the physical body pays the penalty and may show certain shortcomings in those parts which underlie this part of the etheric body. It would follow therefore that in unmistakable cholerics who are true to type the anatomical condition of certain organs corresponding to this part of the etheric body betrays an insufficient development. Read the anatomical findings on a type such as Napoleon and you will be struck by the proof it affords of what I am saying. Only when we begin to study the hidden aspects of human nature shall we really begin to understand these matters.

You may now ask: How does what was said in the last lecture agree with what we have said today? It agrees perfectly. We spoke yesterday of the four temperaments; they are determined by the forces of the etheric body. And, in fact, the life of the etheric body is related to time in the same way as the differentiated structure of the members is related to space. The physical body becomes inwardly more vitally alive in the element of space, differentiating its several members as it were; the etheric body becomes more alive as its members are differentiated in time, that is, when life in time is experienced successively in independent parts and members.

In fact the basic characteristic of the melancholic is that he always bears within him something he has experienced in time, a past experience. He who is able to understand the etheric body of the melancholic finds that it still bears within it the after-vibrations of what it has experienced in the past. I am not now thinking of what was referred to here in the case of the human brain and which relates to primeval times, but of what is usually called melancholy; the etheric life of the head especially is stimulated at a certain time, in youth, let us say: then, what has been stimulated is so strongly influenced that in later life the melancholic still bears in his etheric body the vibrations that were imprinted in his youth, whilst in those who are not melancholic these vibrations have ceased. In the case of the phlegmatic and sanguinic person there is a kind of floating with the stream of time; but in the phlegmatic person there is, as it were, a perfectly steady floating with the stream of time, whilst the sanguine person alternates between a faster or slower reaction to the external stream of time. The choleric person, on the other hand, resists the approach of future time and this is a characteristic feature. He therefore repels time in a certain sense and rapidly rids himself of the vibrations that time evokes in his etheric body. The melancholic person therefore bears within him the greatest number of after-vibrations of past experiences, the choleric person the least. If you recall the somewhat grotesque comparison of the fully inflated ball with the etheric body of the choleric you can use that analogy here. It is difficult for the successive events to make an impression on the ball. It rejects them and therefore does not permit the events working in the steam of time to vibrate strongly in it. Hence the choleric does not bear them for long within him. The melancholic person who allows the events to work deeply into his etheric body has to suffer for a long time the vibrations which he carries with him into the future from the past.

In order to understand the etheric body and the physical body it is well to remember that the physical body is principally a spatial body and the etheric body a temporal being. If we regard the etheric body solely as a spatial being we fail to understand it. The diagram we made is only a kind of pictorial representation in space of the life of the etheric body flowing in the stream of time and adapting itself to the current of time. Because the life of the etheric body itself runs its course in time, is a life in time, we therefore experience time with our etheric body, that is, we experience the external stream of events in time.

When man undergoes occult development he also experiences another stream of events in time. In ordinary life we are scarcely aware of this stream of events, but we shall certainly become more aware of it when the soul is more highly developed: we shall experience the daily cycle, for, in a certain way, the Spirits of the annual cycle also work with lesser forces into the daily cycle. It is the same sun that determines the daily cycle and the annual cycle! He who has undergone an esoteric development will soon find that there exists a similar relationship between his etheric body and what takes place in the external ether, that he will react to the Spirits of morning differently from the Spirits of midday and from those of evening. The Spirits of morning so affect us that we feel, so to speak, more stimulated in our etheric body to an activity which inclines more to the intellect, to reason, an activity which is more capable of reflecting upon what has been experienced and can better assess what has been perceived when we recall it. As midday approaches, these powers of judgement gradually diminish; we feel that inwardly the impulses of the will come more into play. Although our creative powers towards midday are less sustained than in the morning, inwardly the forces of the will are more active. And then towards evening the productive forces manifest themselves, forces that are related more to imagination. Thus the spiritual Beings who send their forces into the life-ether conditions of the earth differ also in relation to the duties they have to perform.

We can rest assured that the more we overcome the materialistic mode of thinking of our time the more we shall understand the need to take into account the adaptation of the etheric body to the element of time. A time will come when we shall find it strange that the morning session in schools will be devoted to a subject that makes special claims upon the imagination. In future we shall find this just as strange as we find it strange today when someone wears a fur coat in August and a light summer costume in winter. These things, it is true, seem a far cry today, but they will come far sooner than people anticipate. A time will come when – taking into account the difference between summer and winter – people will realise that it is absurd to arrange the curriculum in any other way than as follows: several hours in the morning will be devoted to study, the afternoon will be free and then again in the evening several hours will be devoted to study. Given the present school timetable this will hardly seem feasible. But one day it will be found to accord with the exigences of human nature. The morning will be devoted to mathematics, the evening to the reading of poetry. We are now living in an age when an understanding of these things is completely buried under an avalanche of materialism which is now at its height and we shall find that what appears to be most reasonable today will be found to be most foolish when we take into account the whole nature of man.

Another consequence will be that during winter, thanks to esoteric development, we shall feel more and more that we are not so imprisoned in ourselves, within the etheric body, as we are during summer, but that we are more directly united with the Spirit of the Earth. This difference will be felt in such a way that during summer we shall say to ourselves: We are now living with the Spirits who have worked upon us from primordial times, whose work we bear within us, whilst the direct Spirit of the Earth is now farther from us in summer. In winter the inner vibrations, which from ancient times we bear within us, especially in the head, will be less manifest; we shall feel more united with the Spirit of the Earth, we shall realise that the Spirit of the Earth keeps watch in winter. As he sleeps in summer he keeps watch in winter. During summer the Spirit of the Earth sees the burgeoning of the plants just as the sleeping man sees the vegetative forces wake to life in his own body. In winter they withdraw, just as these vegetative forces withdraw during man's waking life. In winter the Spirit of the Earth keeps watch; the earth is united as it were with the waking spirit, just as man during his waking hours is united with his awakened spirit. Consequently, thanks to esoteric development, we begin to feel that in summer we must think and must strive to elaborate our thoughts, but not our inspirations which spring from within, from the independent etheric body. In winter we are more easily inspired with thoughts than in summer, so that in winter human thought works more as an inspiration than in summer. This peculiarly human thinking comes to us so easily in winter that in a certain sense it is spontaneous. Of course these two modes of thinking may be combined in divers ways; they may assume a quite individual form in a particular person, so that if he is more inclined to think thoughts tending towards the supersensible this may be reversed. Through the fact that it is easier in summer to direct one's thoughts towards the supersensible than in winter, it is possible that precisely the reverse may happen. But as regards the experience of the etheric body what I have just said holds good.

The more a person progresses in his esoteric development the more he is sensible of this participation in the life of the external etheric forces. And if he wishes to develop his etheric body in the right way he must first suppress sensory perception and then gradually eliminate thinking also; in particular he must eliminate abstract thinking and gradually proceed to concrete pictorial thinking, then from thinking to thought and finally suspend thought. Then when he has achieved an empty consciousness and suspended his thoughts, in the manner described in the second part of my book *Occult Science – an*

Outline he feels that his normal thinking ceases and that which he had hitherto produced by his own efforts as his thinking dissolves; and in its place he feels himself strangely animated by thoughts that assail him, thoughts that stream into him as though from unknown worlds.

It is a transition in the life of the human soul which can be described by saying – I beg you not to misunderstand the expression – man ceases to be clever and begins to grow wise. A quite definite idea is associated with this. Cleverness that we acquire inwardly through discernment, shrewdness which is an earthly gift disappears. We develop an inner frame of mind which sets little store by them. For we gradually feel kindle within us a wisdom bestowed on us by the gods. I beg you not to misunderstand the expression, for this experience enables us to use this expression without presumption and in all humility and modesty. In the face of wisdom bestowed by the gods man becomes increasingly more humble; he is defiantly proud only of his own cleverness and his so-called intelligence.

Then when he undergoes this experience, he gradually feels as if this wisdom, this heaven-sent wisdom, is streaming into his etheric body and filling it. This is a very important experience, for he undergoes this experience in a particular manner; he feels life to be carried along with the stream of time. But the stream of wisdom is something that comes towards him, something which, as he floats with the stream of time pours into him like an advancing stream. In fact he feels this influx – speaking figuratively – as streams, but streams existing in time which enter through the head, pour into the body and are absorbed by the body.

What I have just described gradually assumes the character of a very definite experience. We no longer feel ourselves to be in space, for we learn to feel our etheric body which is a temporal body; we learn to move in the element of time, but at the same time we learn continually to meet, as it were, the spiritual Beings who approach us from the other side of the cosmos, who come towards us from the future and bestow wisdom upon us. The feeling of receiving this wisdom can only be attained when

LECTURE FOUR

esoteric or occult development has been so ordered that we have developed in ourselves a feeling that prepares the soul to meet all future contingencies: when we have developed serenity towards all that the future may bring us, that is, the future experiences that life may have in store for us. If we still face these experiences with strong feelings of sympathy and antipathy, if we have not yet learnt to take our Karma seriously, that is, to accept with equanimity what Karma brings, then we are not yet able to have that peculiar understanding for the wisdom that streams towards us, for only through experience accepted with serenity can we distinguish these luminous currents of wisdom that penetrate our being. The experience just described indicates a definite stage in our esoteric experience, the stage at which we arrive, and which we can only really experience when we accept every trial which befalls us with gratitude and serenity. The transformation of our etheric body which takes place in true esoteric development enables us to do this, for in addition to other exigences of esoteric development it demands that we acquire serenity and a true understanding of our Karma so that we do not through sympathy and antipathy attract what Karma has in store for us, or rebel against the blows of fate, but that we learn to accept our Karma with equanimity. This acceptance of Karma forms part of our esoteric development and it is this which makes it possible for us so to transform our etheric body that it gradually learns to be aware more and more of the external etheric life surrounding it.

LECTURE FIVE

The Hague, 24 March 1913

It is important for us to consider this cycle of lectures in the right way. They are a description of the experiences which a person undergoes in the form of transformations within himself during his esoteric development or associated with his anthroposophical work, so that what we have described is to be looked upon as something that can actually be experienced during development. Of course only the most striking, the most typical experiences can be discussed; but from the description of these cardinal experiences we shall be able to form an idea of many other things which call for observation in the course of our development. Yesterday we spoke of the fact that the neophyte acquires a greater sensitivity towards what is taking place in the external life ether or in the ether as a whole. These experiences are connected with many others, and we should pay particular attention to the experience we have in relation to our faculty of judgement.

As human beings standing in the world we cannot help passing judgement upon whatever befalls us; we form our own ideas about things and pronounce one thing to be right, another to be wrong. A person's capacity for judging things depends, as a rule, upon what is called intelligence, shrewdness, discernment; but in the course of development we gradually see these capacities in a different light. This question was touched upon yesterday. We find more and more that in matters concerned with the higher spiritual life, this shrewdness or cleverness is not of the slightest value, although we need a fund of shrewdness or common sense if we wish to embark upon the path to the higher worlds. And thus we find ourselves in a situation that may easily appear intolerable to the utilitarian, namely that what is vitally necessary at first for our higher development loses its value when we have attained this higher development. We must do our utmost therefore to develop here on the physical plane sound judgement which weighs the facts objectively; but at the same time we must clearly understand that during our sojourn in the spiritual worlds this capacity for judgement has not the same value as on the physical plane. If we wish to develop higher senses that are healthy and balanced we must start from sound judgement; but for higher vision this healthy power of judgement must be transformed into healthy vision.

No matter how far advanced our development may be, so long as we have to live on the physical plane we belong, as human beings, to this plane and on this plane our task is to cultivate a sound capacity for judgement. Therefore we must see to it that we learn in good time not to confuse life in the higher worlds with life on the physical plane. He who wishes to apply directly to the physical plane his experiences of the higher worlds easily becomes an unpractical visionary. We must accustom ourselves to be able to live wholly on the spiritual plane and then, when we return to the physical plane, to adhere as firmly as possible to what is appropriate to this plane. We must fulfil carefully and conscientiously this dual role demanded by the dual nature of our spiritual and physical life. In this domain we must learn to develop a right relation to the world by doing our utmost to avoid mingling what really belongs to the higher worlds with everyday life and to avoid saying as far as possible, which we may be easily tempted to do when we dislike something in a person: that we cannot endure his aura. It is better to keep to the language of everyday life and simply to say: I find such and such to be distasteful. In this respect it is better to be down to earth and to use as little as possible in everyday life expressions which are right and justified in relation to the higher life. We ought carefully to refrain from employing in daily life words, concepts and ideas which belong to the higher life. This may seem perhaps a pedantic demand to anyone who, out of enthusiasm for the spiritual life, finds it necessary to permeate his whole being with this spiritual life; and yet, what in ordinary life may seem pedantic is an important principle of training for the higher worlds.

Therefore, even if it should seem more natural to us to describe ordinary life in terms that belong to the higher life, let us translate them into a language most suited to the physical plane! It must be emphasised again and again that those things are not unimportant, but are significant and far-reaching in their effect. Once this is admitted we can say without hesitation that in relation to life in the higher worlds ordinary judgement is of little consequence and we begin to feel that the way in which we used our intelligence before must now cease. And again we perceive – this is an experience that becomes increasingly more frequent – that we are dependent upon the etheric life of the world, that is, upon time. How often do we find at the present time, that people from their early years begin to criticise everything and imagine that when they have acquired a certain capacity for judgement they can dogmatise about everything and can philosophise on anything and everything. Esoteric development totally demolishes this pretension to be able to philosophise on all kinds of subjects, for we are then made aware that our judgements have a solid foundation that needs to mature. We learn to recognise that if we wish to arrive at a judgement with which we can agree we must live for a time with certain ideas we have acquired, so that our etheric body can come to terms with them. We find that we must wait before we can arrive at a sure judgement. Only then do we realise the full significance of these words: to allow what is in the soul to mature. And fundamentally we become more and more modest.

Now the strange thing about this acquisition of modesty is that it is not always possible to hold the balance between the occasion when it is necessary to pronounce an immediate judgement and the occasion when we are able to wait for maturity before passing an opinion, because it is precisely in these matters that we can delude ourselves to a large extent and only the experience of life itself can enlighten us. Let us suppose a philosopher raises the question of some cosmic mystery or cosmic law with someone who has reached a certain degree of esoteric development. If he can only fall back upon his philosophical judgement he will be convinced that he must be right on some point or other and we can understand that he must hold this belief. But the other person will be quite aware that the question cannot be solved with the kind of judgement advanced by the philosopher, for he knows that the ideas which determine the philosopher's judgement he himself entertained in former times, that he allowed them to mature in him and that this first enabled him to have an opinion on the question; he knows that he has lived with this question and thereby has matured sufficiently to pass the judgement which he now pronounces at a higher stage of maturity. But an understanding between the two is really out of the question and in many cases cannot be established immediately; it can only be established if there awakens in the philosopher a feeling that it is necessary to allow certain things to mature in his soul before he permits himself to give an opinion about them. We must recognise more and more that opinions and views, our way of looking at things, must be striven for, must be acquired by persistent effort. We develop a deep and intense feeling for this because we have acquired this inner feeling for time which fundamentally is connected with the development of the etheric body.

Indeed, we gradually perceive that a certain opposition arises in the soul between the way in which we judged formerly and the way in which we judge now after having attained a certain maturity on the subject in question. We notice that these two modes of judgement are like two opposing forces and we then notice a certain inner mobility of the temporal in ourselves and that our earlier judgements must be modified by later judgements. This is the dawning in the consciousness of a certain feeling for time created by the existence of inner conflicts which can only arise through a certain opposition between the earlier and the later judgements. It is absolutely necessary to develop an inner feeling, an inner perception of time, for we must realise that we can only experience the etheric when we acquire an inner conception of time.

Furthermore we always have the feeling that the earlier judgement originates in ourselves, in our cognition, that the later judgement has seemingly flowed into us, has been poured into us, as it were, has been bestowed upon us. The feeling of what was described in the last lecture becomes increasingly clear: that the cleverness which originates in ourselves must be replaced by the wisdom derived from a kind of surrender to a stream coming from the future. To feel oneself filled with thoughts, in contradistinction to what we thought before when we believed we were the architects of our own thoughts, that is the mark of progress. When we begin to feel more and more that we no longer create our thoughts, but that the thoughts think themselves in us, this feeling is a sign that the etheric body is gradually developing the necessary inner feeling of time. All our earlier thoughts will savour of egoism; everything that we have acquired in the course of maturing will savour of burning up, of consuming our self-created thoughts. And thus the gradual transformation of our inner being ends in a strange experience: we become increasingly aware that our own thinking, our own thought processes must be suppressed because they are of little value; what is of real value is our surrender to the thoughts that stream into us from the cosmos.

Our own life loses, as it were, a part of itself – and this is extremely important – it loses the part we prefer to call personal thinking, and there only remains personal, perceiving feeling and willing. These also undergo a transformation at the same time as the thinking. We are no longer the architects of our own thoughts, but they think themselves within us. With the feeling that the thoughts have their own forces by means of which they think themselves is associated a certain merging of feeling and will. Feeling, it could be said, becomes more and more active and the will becomes more and more permeated with feeling. Feeling and will become more closely related to each other than they were before on the physical plane; we cannot express any impulse of the will without a feeling being associated with it.

LECTURE FIVE

Many of our actions provoke in us a bitter feeling, others a feeling of exaltation. When we become aware of our will we experience at the same time a deeper comprehension of our own will impulses, we become the arbiter of our will impulses. We gradually find that pleasurable feelings which are aroused merely for the sake of their satisfaction invite a certain reproach; but those which are so felt that one says: the human soul must provide a field of action for these feelings, these must be experienced inwardly, otherwise they would not exist in the universe – such feelings we gradually find to be more legitimate than the others.

Here let me give a typical example, a radical example in fact, which illustrates what I mean. Someone – I have no wish to decry anything, but simply to express the matter somewhat radically – someone with every justification might enjoy a good meal. When he experiences this pleasure, it is undeniable that something happens in him, but it makes little difference to the universe, to the cosmos, whether the individual in question enjoys a good meal or not; it is of no consequence to life in general. But if someone takes up the Gospel of St. John and reads only three or four lines of it, that is of immense importance to the cosmos; for if, amongst all the souls on earth nobody were to read St. John's Gospel, the whole mission of the earth could not be fulfilled. Through our participation in these activities there stream forth spiritually the forces which provide ever new life to the earth to replace the dying life.

We must distinguish between the experience which is a purely egoistic feeling and that in which we simply provide a stage for a feeling that is necessary for the existence of the world. Under certain circumstances a man may be able to do very little externally, but if he knows, not for the sake of personal enjoyment, but thanks to his psychic development, that through his feeling an opportunity is provided for the existence of this feeling which is important for the existence of the world, then he thereby achieves something that is a valuable addition to the world. Let me add the following, strange as it may seem: There was once a Greek philosopher called Plato who wrote many books. As long as we live only on the physical plane in our soul life, we read him for instruction. This external instruction is important for the physical plane; it is desirable to make use of every means of instruction on the physical plane otherwise we remain ignorant. The things achieved on the physical plane are there for our instruction. But when the soul has developed esoterically we take up the works of Plato and read them again for a different reason, because Plato and his works only have a meaning in terrestrial life if what he has created is also experienced in the souls of men; and then we read him not only for instruction, but because thereby something of positive value to the world is achieved.

Thus we must cultivate something in our feeling which enables us to distinguish between egoistic feeling that tends more towards lotus eating and selfless feeling that appears to us as a spiritual duty. This may extend even into external life and the external conception of life. And here we touch upon a question which, one might say, from personal experience throws light upon social life. When a person who is familiar with the secrets of esotericism observes the world and its ways, when he sees how so many people waste their leisure time instead of ennobling their feelings with the gifts of spiritual creations, he could weep at man's stupidity which ignores all that life offers and which could permeate human feeling and human experience. And in this domain it is necessary to draw attention to the fact that when these experiences begin a certain more subtle egoism will manifest itself in human nature. In the following lectures we shall see how this more refined egoism has a tendency to conquer itself; but at first it manifests itself as a more subtle egoism and in the course of our spiritual development we shall be able to experience personally a kind of need for spiritual nourishment, a thirst for things of the spirit. And grotesque as it may sound, it is nevertheless true that a person who undergoes esoteric development may say, from a certain stage onwards, without indulging in pride or vanity, that all the spiritual creations on earth are there to be enjoyed by him. That is as it should be. And gradually he is drawn towards these spiritual delights. In this respect esotericism will not cause any mischief in the world, for one can rest assured that when this thirst for the spiritual creations of mankind manifests itself, it will do no harm.

As a result of this something else becomes evident. We gradually feel our etheric body awakening because we attach little importance to our own thinking, we regard it as something inferior compared with the thoughts pouring into us from the cosmos that is interwoven with the divine. We feel more and more that will and feeling are self created, that egoity affirms itself only in our will and feeling, whilst the gifts of wisdom with which we feel ourselves to be permeated are perceived as something that unites us with the whole cosmos. This experience is then associated with another; we begin to feel that this inner activity of feeling and will is impregnated with sympathy and antipathy. We become ever more sensitively aware that it is shameful to behave in a certain way because we have been endowed with a certain measure of wisdom. On the other hand we may feel that it is right and proper to act as we do because we are aware of this measure of wisdom vouchsafed us. An experience of self-control manifesting itself in the sphere of feeling follows naturally. A bitter feeling overtakes us when we feel arising independently of us a will impelling us to do what is not justified in view of the wisdom in which we have participated. It is in connection with what we have said that we perceive most clearly this bitter feeling; and it is important that the neophyte should not ignore the fact that in this respect the whole inner life of feeling can be refined. In exoteric life when a person has spoken, has said something or other, he thinks no more about it, whereas the person who has undergone an esoteric development has a conscience over what he has said; he feels something akin to an inner shame when he has said something that is unwarranted from a moral or intellectual point of view. He feels something like a sort of gratitude – not self approval – when he has been able to express something to which the wisdom he has acquired can assent. And if he feels – and for this too one develops a delicate sensitivity – a certain inner self-satisfaction, a certain self-complaisance when he has said something that is right, then that is a sign that he is consumed with vanity and this in no way serves his development. He thus learns to distinguish between the feeling of satisfaction of having said something with which one can agree and the self-complaisance which is worthless. We must try not to allow this latter feeling to arise, but only to develop a feeling of shame when we have said something untrue or a-moral, and a feeling of gratitude for the wisdom bestowed on us and which we cannot claim as our own, for it is a gift from the universe, a feeling of gratitude that we have succeeded in saying something befitting this wisdom.

Gradually we begin to feel the same thing in relation to our own thinking. As we have already said, we must keep our feet firmly on the physical plane. Whilst we must not attach too much importance to our self-created thoughts, we must nonetheless continue to develop them; but this personal thinking is now transformed also, and indeed in such a way that we submit it to the self-control we have just described. If we can say of a thought that it is our own creation and is in keeeping with the wisdom vouchsafed us, then we develop a feeling of gratitude towards this wisdom. On the other hand a thought which is erroneous, unseemly or a-moral is accompanied by an inner feeling of shame and we feel: Can I still be like this? Is it still possible that I am so egotistic as to think these thoughts in spite of the wisdom bestowed on me? – It is most important to feel this kind of self-control in one's inner being. The peculiarity of this self-control is that it never arises through the critical intellect, but that it always manifests itself in us in feeling, in the sentient life.

Let us pay careful attention to the following: A person who is only intelligent, who only applies his critical judgement to the external world, can never understand what is involved here, for it must arise in the feeling. When he has developed this feeling, when this feeling arises as if from his own inner being, he identifies himself with this feeling of shame or gratitude and feels that his self is united with this feeling. And if I were to represent schematically what is thus experienced I would say that we have the feeling of wisdom streaming in from above, coming towards us from above, streaming into our head from the front and filling us from top to bottom. On the other hand we feel as though there streams towards us from our own body a feeling of shame; we identify ourselves with this feeling and recognise the wisdom which is present as something bestowed from without. We then feel within ourselves a region where this feeling, which is now the ego, meets this instreaming wisdom bestowed upon us. When we experience inwardly the region where these two streams meet, we have the right inner experience of the etheric world. We experience the thoughts

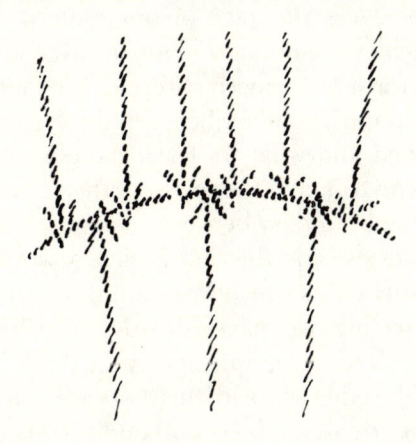

pressing in from the external etheric world – for it is the wisdom streaming towards us from this external etheric world that presses in upon us and is perceived by means of these two feelings. Such is the etheric world when rightly perceived, and when we perceive it in this way we mount towards the higher Beings who only descend as far as the etheric body and not as far as the physical body. On the other hand it is possible to experience this etheric world in a certain sense in a wrong way. We experience it correctly when thinking and feeling meet as we have just described. The experience therefore is a purely inner process in the soul. The elementary or etheric world may be experienced incorrectly if we experience it on the boundary between respiration and our own etheric body. If we practise breathing exercises too early in our training or incorrectly, we gradually witness our own respiration. Through the perception of the breathing process of which we are unaware in normal respiration it is possible to develop a respiration which is conscious of itself. And with this experience may be associated a certain perception of the etheric world. By means of all kinds of breathing exercises one may observe and experience etheric processes which are real in the external world, but which belong to the lowest external psychic processes, etheric processes which, if experienced too early, will never provide a true idea of the real spiritual world.

Of course at a certain stage of our esoteric exercises it is possible to achieve voluntary control over our breathing process, but it must be properly directed. We then perceive the etheric world on the boundary between thinking and feeling as already described and what we learn there is only confirmed because we come to know the grosser etheric processes which take place on the boundary between the etheric world and our breathing processes. For the fact is that a world of genuine higher spirituality exists which we attain through that union of wisdom and feeling we have already described; there we penetrate to the deeds accomplished by the Beings of the higher Hierarchies in the etheric world. But there are a large number of elemental beings of all kinds – good and bad, hostile, hideous and harmful – which, if we encounter them at the wrong time, obtrude themselves upon us as if they really constituted a significant spiritual world, whilst they are nothing more than the lowest dregs of the spiritual world. He who wishes to penetrate into the spiritual world must also become acquainted with these entities; but it is inadvisable to come in contact with them early in one's training. For, strangely enough, if we first make their acquaintance without having trod the thorny path of our own inner experience, we develop a fondness for them, a marked predilection for them. And it may happen that a person who raises himself in the wrong way, especially through a physical training which entails a modification of the breathing processes, will describe certain things pertaining to this spiritual world as they appear to him. He describes them in such a way that many people take them for something extremely beautiful, whilst the person who perceives them intuitively may find them hideous and loathsome. Such things are quite possible when we experience the spiritual world.

There is no need to speak here of other methods which a person may practise and through which he may enter into evil worlds. In occultism it is customary not to speak of what may be regarded as the dregs of this spiritual world. It is not necessary to enter this world and therefore it is not usual to speak of the methods which interrupt the breathing process. For the breathing process, if it is not used in the right way, leads inevitably to the lower beings whom we must certainly come to know one day, but not to begin with, because otherwise they would exercise a certain seductive power over us which they ought not to have. We shall only acquire a genuinely objective point of view with regard to their value when we have penetrated into the spiritual world by another path.

If we now begin to feel streaming out of us, as it were, in response to the wisdom bestowed on us, feelings of shame, feelings of gratitude, if these feelings are thrown up by our own organism, we thereby first become acquainted in the most elementary way with something of which we must learn more in the course of our further esoteric development. We pointed out yesterday that through the gradual experience of the etheric we come to know the Amshaspands of the teaching of Zarathustra, which are active in the etheric body of our brain. From our point of view we can also say that we acquire there, in the first instance, an idea of the activity of the Archangels, of what these Archangels have to do in us. Through what is dammed up here, through the feelings of gratitude and shame which arise in us here and which bear the stamp of our personality because they originate in us, we receive the first elementary true conception of what are called the Archai or Primal Forces; for what the Archangels realise in us we first experience in the most elementary way, as we have already described. Whilst we first experience in the head – when we begin to experience etherically – the Archangels and their activities in a shadowy way, in the organic system into which wisdom penetrates and which produces a reaction in us, we experience the Archai, the Primal Forces, impregnated with an element of will, yet not quite of a volitional nature, which have entered into us and work in the human personality. When we learn to feel in this way we gradually acquire an idea of what the occultist means when he speaks of the original incarnation of our earth on Old Saturn where the Primal Forces or Spirits of Personality lived at their human stage, so to speak. At that time these Spirits of Personality were "human". They have developed further and in so doing have acquired the capacity to work from the supersensible world. And how do they exercise at the present time, in our present earth epoch, this power that they have acquired now that their evolution has progressed to the point where they can intervene on earth?

They are now able so to work from the supersensible upon our corporeal nature, upon our sheath, that they evoke in our etheric body forces which manifest in the manner described. They have directed these forces into us, and if we feel today that we are so organised that we can develop in ourselves the feelings, already described, of gratitude and shame as an inner natural process (and it is possible to experience this), then we must say: In order that this can become an inner experience, in order that our etheric body may pulsate and respond to the wisdom in this way, to this end the Archai have poured forces into our etheric body. In the same way man himself in future incarnations of our earth will one day be able to imprint into the inner being of other entities inferior to him similar capacities in order that they may develop a sheath corresponding to our own. What we are destined to know of the spiritual worlds will gradually be gained through inner experience, by our passing over from physical experience to etheric experience. On Old Saturn as you know – I refer to this once again in order to clarify matters – warmth was the densest physical condition, the only physical condition which had been reached by the middle of the Saturn epoch. And you can read in my book *Occult Science – An Outline* that the Saturn activities in the physical were currents of heat and cold. We can describe these currents psychically, from the aspect of the soul, by saying: The warmth which streamed forth was the gratitude of the Spirits of Personality and the cold which streamed forth in another direction was the feeling of shame of the same Spirits of Personality. What we must gradually acquire is the capacity to merge the physical activity with the moral activity for the further we penetrate into the higher worlds, the more these two principles are connected – the physical aspect which has ceased to be physical and the moral which then flows through the world with the power of the laws of nature.

Everything that has just been described manifests itself in inner experience through the transformation of the etheric body; at the same time it provokes something else in the human soul – the human soul gradually begins to feel a certain unease that we are largely individual beings, isolated personalities. It is important to be aware of this and it is a good thing to make it a rule to be aware of it. The less interest one has developed (before this stage of esoteric development) in what concerns mankind in general, in the everyday needs of mankind, the more disturbing we find this as we progress. A person who has shown no interest in the needs of mankind and who none the less would like to pursue an esoteric development would feel more and more a burden to himself. A person, for example, who is able to go through life without sympathy for the sufferings of others or participative joy in their joy, who cannot enter into the souls of others, such a person, when he progresses in esoteric development, feels himself to be a kind of burden. If we none the less pursue an esoteric development despite the fact that we remain indifferent to human joy and sorrow, we become a heavy burden to ourselves. And we can be quite sure that our esoteric development will remain a purely superficial and intellectual affair, that we shall accept spiritual teaching like the recipes of a cookery book or the theories of physical science so long as we are not conscious of this burden, if, in spite of our development, we cannot develop compassion for the sufferings of mankind and share in their joy and gladness.

It is important therefore to widen our human interests during occult development, and there is nothing worse than to fail to try, as we progress, to gain an understanding of every kind of human feeling, human experience and human life. That does not mean of course – and this must be emphasised again and again – that we must silently ignore the wrong-doing in the world, for that would be an injustice towards the world. It means something else. Whereas, before esoteric development we may have felt a certain pleasure in finding fault with some human failing, this pleasure in criticising others ceases entirely in the course of esoteric development. We are all familiar with the cynic who delights in delivering a pertinent criticism of the faults of others. Not that healthy criticism of human failings should cease, nor should we in all circumstances condemn an attitude such as that of Erasmus of Rotterdam in his *Praise of Folly*. One may be perfectly entitled to be severely critical of the wrong-doings of the world; but in the case of a person who undergoes an esoteric development every reproach, every word of censure he utters or translates into deeds causes him pain, and promises to bring increasing pain. And the sorrow at being obliged to find fault is something that may serve as a barometer of esoteric development. The more we can still feel pleasure when we are obliged to find fault or when we find the world ridiculous, the less we are really ready to progress. We must gradually acquire a sort of understanding that there is developing in us more and more a living process that makes us look upon the follies and frailties of the world now with humour, now with tears, with detachment or with sorrow. This inner separation, this independence from what was formerly chaotically commingled, also forms part of the transformation that the etheric body of man undergoes.

LECTURE SIX

The Hague, 25 March 1913

We have considered the modifications in the physical body and the etheric body of man in so far as they are experienced by him in the course of the estoeric development he endeavours to pursue. If we wish to describe the fundamental character of these modifications we can say that in the course of his development man is more and more aware inwardly of his physical body and his etheric body. In relation to the physical body we have emphasised that the several organs become increasingly independent the more the aspirant progresses, that they become to some extent more independent of each other. The physical body is felt, one might say, to be inwardly more alive; the etheric body, as we pointed out, not only feels more alive, but in general becomes more sensitive; and is permeated with a kind of consciousness, for it begins to respond to the course of external events with a subtle sensitivity. We pointed out also that in the course of esoteric development man becomes more sensitive to the seasonal changes of spring, summer, autumn and winter; they become for him something sharply defined so that the successive temporal events are more detached, more insulated from one another than is the case in normal life; they become separate and distinct.

We can say therefore that man begins, as it were, to experience the processes in the external ether. This is the first step in a real liberation from his bodily nature. He thus becomes increasingly independent of his own body and so begins to participate in the world around him. He begins to experience spring, summer, autumn and winter within himself, as it were; but because he lives more in the external world, he ceases to live in his own body. Now we emphasised yesterday that all this is related to the fact that we become more sensitive to our own corporeal nature. As we begin to be more independent of our physical body we gradually perceive it to be a kind of embarrassment; we notice that everything that relates only to our own corporeality becomes a kind of reproach. And we have made a great step forward in higher development when, thanks to the ideas and experiences described yesterday, we begin to be no longer wholly in harmony with our own human personality; and when we experience this to an ever greater extent much has been achieved in the furtherance of a higher spiritual experience.

Now in anticipation I will attempt today to depict the further progress of our observations which hitherto have been directed more from within the inner life to the outer life by first trying to describe the point of view of the human being when, with his astral body and his Ego, he has already become independent of his physical and etheric bodies. We will speak of the intermediate states in the following lectures. In order to make this easier to understand I will assume that, during sleep, we experience the moment when we become clairvoyant outside the body and can look back upon our physical and etheric bodies.

So far we have only taken a few steps towards this condition and have reached the point when we have relinquished our body and have learnt to experience, for example, the seasons of the year and the times of the day. We will now consider the situation that would arise if, on the one hand, we had the physical and etheric bodies and the Ego and astral body were released as occurs in sleep. Let us suppose that we could look back upon the physical body and etheric body we have left behind. These bodies would then appear to us in a wholly different light from that of ordinary life. In ordinary life we look at our physical body through the eyes of everyday external observation or of external physical science and, with a certain justification, we consider it to be the crown of terrestrial creation. In this terrestrial creation we distinguish a mineral kingdom, a vegetable kingdom, an animal and a human kingdom; and we see that all the various virtues which are spread over the different animal species are united, so to speak, in this crown of creation, the human body. We shall see that to external physical observation there is a certain justification for this view. The present lecture is not intended to encourage the belief that what at first may be revealed in retrospective observation when we look back upon the physical and etheric bodies, if we were suddenly to become clairvoyant during sleep, would provide any definitive conclusion about the nature of the physical body. The purpose of this lecture is simply to capture, as it were, a moment of clairvoyant retrospective vision. This moment may reveal the following: As we look back, we see initially our etheric body which appears as a completely integrated nebulous structure with divers currents which will be described in more detail later – a beautifully constructed form which is in continuous movement, never still, never at rest in any part; then embedded in this etheric body we see the physical body.

Now remember that we have already said that our thinking must be eliminated. Therefore we preserve an open mind towards what we see in clairvoyant vision, for it is above all a fundamental demand of this clairvoyant vision that we allow ourselves to be wholly inspired by the cosmic thoughts that stream into us. We meditate therefore upon what we see there; but this acts especially upon our feeling, it influences our feeling and our will. When we have really attained the detachment we spoke of earlier we seem to have lost our own mode of thinking. And so with the feeling that is peculiar to us we look back upon what is embedded in that ever mobile nebulous structure of our etheric body, namely, our physical body.

We first receive a general impression, and this general impression is such that what we perceive fills us with infinite sadness, terrible sadness. And this spirit pervading the soul, this mood of sadness is not associated with any particular individual; it is common to all. There is not a single person who, when looking back from without in the manner described upon his physical body as it is embedded in the etheric body, is not overwhelmed with infinite sadness. All the impressions that I am now describing are clearly expressed at first in the feelings, not in the field of thoughts. Infinite sadness, a profound melancholy overcomes us when we look up to the world of cosmic thoughts that stream into us. These thoughts which are not our own, but which are the creative thoughts weaving and working in the world, throw light upon this structure of our physical body, and by the way they illuminate it, tell us what it really is that we see there.

They tell us that what we see is the last decadent survival of a long vanished splendour. And through what these thoughts tell us we receive the impression that our physical body is something that once was mighty and glorious, but is now withered and shrivelled; its former majestic splendour is now no more than a tiny shrunken form. That which is embedded in our etheric body appears to us as a last memory crystallised in the physical of a vanished primordial splendour. We see the various physical organs which today constitute our digestive, circulatory and respiratory systems. We look at them from without, observing them spiritually, and they appear to us in such a way that we say: All things present in the physical body are the shrivelled, desiccated survivals of living beings which once existed, beings which lived in a splendid environment and are now shrivelled up and withered. And the life animating the lungs, the heart, the liver and the other organs today is only the last decadent manifestation of a one-time powerful inner life.

In this clairvoyant vision the organs gradually assume the form they once possessed. Just as a long forgotten thought, when we make the effort to recall it, grows into what it once was, so too that which we bear within us as the lungs, for example, and which appears at first as the last memory of a vanished majesty and splendour, grows and increases when seen clairvoyantly. We feel that this experience recalls a distant memory like a present thought which recaptures the experience of its former state. In our clairvoyant vision the lungs develop into the Imagination of that which was once known to the occultist as an accepted symbol and which he still knows today as a symbol of the human form – into the Imagination of the Eagle. We have the feeling that these lungs were at one time a being – they must not be identified with the eagle as we know it today, for this eagle also represents from another angle a decadent survival of a former mighty being which in occultism is designated as the Eagle. As if in a cosmic memory the occultist identifies himself with the Eagle that once existed. And when in retrospect we turn to our heart, we feel too that this appears as a withered and shrivelled survival, as a memory of a former splendour; and we then feel as though we had returned to primordial times, to a being of a remote past which the occultist designates as the Lion. And then the organs of the lower part of the body appear as a memory of what is called in occultism the Bull, a primeval being which formerly lived in majestic surroundings, a being that has become desiccated and shrivelled in the course of evolution and which manifests itself today under the aspect of the organs of the lower part of the body.

I would like therefore to illustrate with the help of a diagram that which once existed and which we discover when we observe

clairvoyantly our corporeal organs from without: we see the Eagle, the Lion and the Bull superposed as in the diagram above. Thus we perceive what once lived in the primeval past as three sublime living beings. (I am only drawing them schematically on a somewhat smaller scale.) Round these principal organs we can also see other organs as they formerly were in the far-distant past. And what we perceive clairvoyantly in this way can be compared to almost all the forms of the animal kingdom on earth.

If we now turn our attention once again to the physical body embedded in the etheric body and observe what is called physiologically the nervous system, this nervous system also appears as a shrivelled, dried up product. But the nervous system which at present is embedded in the physical body appears to the retrospective clairvoyant vision as a collection of wonderful plant-like beings embedded in the etheric body which thread their way in various ways through these entities known by animal names, so that we see a network of plant-like entities extending in all directions. The whole nervous system resolves itself into a collection of primitive plant-like entities, so that we actually see something akin to a plant growth spreading widely in which dwell the animal beings of which we have spoken. As already mentioned, I am speaking of what is seen by the clairvoyant vision which has been described as arising in a condition similar to sleep, that is when, from without, we look at the physical body embedded in the etheric body.

When we see all this before us, we then say to ourselves – because cosmic thoughts give us this information to a certain extent and interpret what lies before us – we then say: Everything that, as a human being, I bear within myself is the withered and shrivelled remnant of what is now disclosed to me clairvoyantly as a cosmic memory. It is important to hasten our development so that we can exercise continual self-control, continual self-knowledge. This self-knowledge enables us at this stage to feel and to reflect: I am outside my physical body. What appeared to me as my physical body embedded in the etheric body has been transformed in my clairvoyant vision into what we have just described. What I now behold no longer exists, it must have existed in a remote past in order that my physical body here on earth could be created. In order that this shrivelled survival could be created, what I now see before me with my clairvoyant vision must once have existed. The physical body makes at first this sad impression because we recognise that it is the last withered survival of a former splendour now disclosed to clairvoyant vision.

If we have brought our self-knowledge to this degree of development, then we become aware that in this astral body which is now outside the physical and etheric bodies we cannot do otherwise. I beg you not to misunderstand me, I am describing the facts and you will see how these facts explain themselves, they resound to the honour of the wise guides of the world; we must first acquaint ourselves with the facts and in the following lectures what is in question will become clear. . . . We cannot do otherwise when we are in the astral body than accept the fact that we are absolute egotists, wholly self centred, and we learn to recognise that there are grounds enough for sadness. For we now feel the urge to know the reason for what has happened, why everything has degenerated.

And the question is: who is to blame for this degeneration? And the form which I see clairvoyantly before me, this wonderful plant being with the perfect animal-like structure within it, who has made it into the present shrivelled human body? Then like an inner inspiration these words ring out: You have brought this upon yourself, you yourself are responsible. And, that you have become what you are now, you owe to the fact that you had the power to impregnate all this splendour with your own being. And because your being infiltrated like poison into this ancient splendour, this former splendour is now reduced to its present shrivelled state.

It is we ourselves therefore who are responsible and we owe the possibility of being a self such as we are today to the fact that we ourselves sowed the seeds of death in all this splendour and so impregnated it that it shrivelled up. Just as a giant tree growing in all its majesty and nourishing divers animals which are entirely dependent upon it, if injected at a certain place dries up, withers and shrivels up from that point, and with it die all the beings nourished by it, so the shrivelled condition of the physical human body is disclosed to our clairvoyant vision. Such is the overpowering impression evoked by this moment of perception and the neophyte feels an increasing urge in his astral body to know how this came about. At this moment there appears to him, worming his way amongst the primordial animal beings which he perceives, so to speak, at the back of the Paradise Garden the wondrous form of Lucifer himself!

Here for the first time through clairvoyant observation we make the acquaintance of Lucifer and we now know: Such were the forces, which today are shrivelled up in the physical human body, at a time when Lucifer appeared within this total cosmic being which is now visible to our clairvoyant vision.

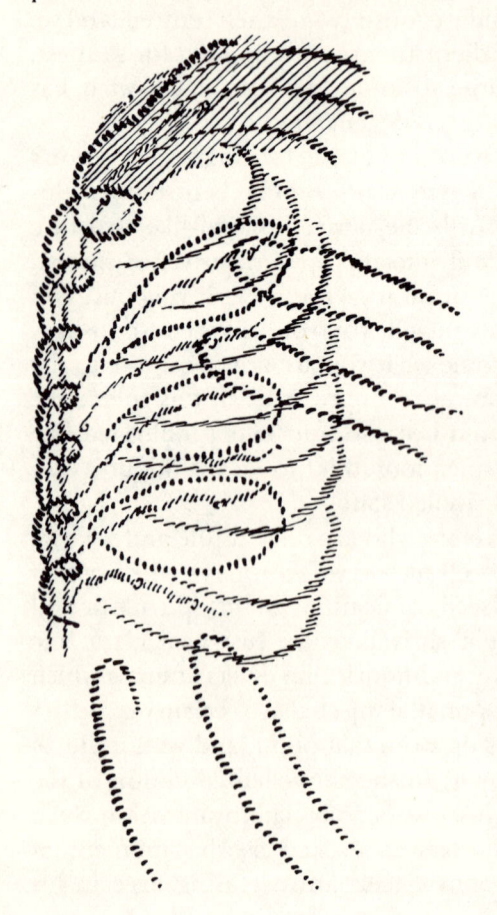

And now man knows that he was present in that far-distant past when what is now disclosed to his clairvoyant vision was a reality: and he knows that he then felt himself to be vitally alive, for he belonged to this world; that was his kingdom. And in this kingdom Lucifer drew man to himself, man united himself with Lucifer. In consequence the Beings of the higher Hierarchies pressed in from behind in streams of force which could be indicated by these lines (see diagram) and forced out the human being who had united himself with Lucifer into these areas towards the front of the head. All this is disclosed to clairvoyant perception. In this area (above on the right) apertures were formed which, in the process of shrinking have become our present sensory organs. The human being who had previously lived in this area was expelled through these apertures because he had united himself with Lucifer. Having been expelled, he now lives in the world outside this structure which has shrunk and become the physical body.

In order that you may form a clear picture, imagine the present physical body becoming larger and larger, all the organs becoming larger, the organs of digestion, circulation and respiration developing into these powerful living animal beings, and the nervous system becoming plant-like beings: and in this mighty configuration picture man as sovereign. On the one hand Lucifer now appears; and because the human being is attracted by Lucifer, Beings of the higher Hierarchies press in from behind and expel the human being out. And because the human being is thus expelled the whole structure gradually shrinks to the small compass occupied by the human body today, and the human being with his entire waking consciousness is outside the body. He has been expelled through the apertures which are now the sense-organs: he is now in the phenomenal world and the world in which he dwelt in the far distant past is now shrivelled up and constitutes his inner organs.

I have now given you an idea of how, through clairvoyant observation, the human being arrives at what is called Paradise. It was in the Mystery schools that the adept directed the thoughts of men towards Paradise. Where was Paradise? people ask. Paradise was to be found in a world which obviously no longer exists in the phenomenal world today. Paradise has shrunk and has multiplied, has become a multiplicity of human beings; the inner organs of the physical body have been left behind as the last memory of Paradise, but the human being has been expelled and no longer lives in his inner being. He can only come to know them by means of clairvoyance, as we have seen. He is aware of the external world, of what is before his eyes, he is familiar with the sounds which impinge upon his ears; formerly he was aware of what was within: but this inner world was grandiose, it was Paradise.

Try now to form an idea of how man, because he is a being whose consciousness extends over the phenomenal world, actually compressed the world in which he dwelt before he entered the phenomenal world into the degenerate product of the inner organs of his body. The Beings who first expelled man and who subsequently worked upon him then made use of Ahriman and other spirits whose activity they transformed into good, adding the limbs, hands, feet and here the face to the etheric torso, thus enabling man by means of his hands, feet, and by means of what is directed inwards through his sense organs, to make use of this shrivelled up Paradise.

We have thus seen in spiritual vision the physical human body enlarged to gigantic proportions, this body which in its present condition represents the shrivelled product of the Paradise of former times. When we observe this we can gain some slight idea of the way in which clairvoyant vision really unfolds. We saw how, at first, man becomes increasingly sensitive in relation to his physical and etheric bodies, and we say, in anticipation, what sort of impressions we receive when from outside his body man looks back upon his physical body embedded in the etheric body. I said that the etheric body is itself in continual movement. When seen from outside nothing is really stationary, everything is in continual movement. Something is continually taking place and the more we learn through spiritual training to observe what is happening there, the wider becomes the tableau of these happenings, and everything takes on meaning. Just as the physical body becomes, so to speak, the true Garden of Paradise, so what takes place in the etheric body becomes processes full of meaning. We will now attempt to describe clearly the facts and processes which we observe when we study the etheric body and leave the physical body out of consideration. Now the physical body as I have described it could only be seen clairvoyantly if we were suddenly awakened to clairvoyance in the deepest sleep; then the physical body would expand to this configuration which I have described. But the etheric body in a certain sense can be more easily seen. It can be seen if we try in a certain way to seize the moment of falling asleep, to seize it so that we do not immediately pass over into unconsciousness but remain conscious for a time after having, with the astral body and the Ego, relinquished the physical and etheric bodies. We then look down principally upon the etheric body and see the movements of the etheric body in the form of vivid dreams. We then see ourselves separated, as by a deep abyss, from what is taking place in the etheric body; but we now see everything happening not in space, but in time. When we are outside our etheric body we must therefore perceive these experiences of movement in the etheric body as if we had consciously slipped back into it again.

We must feel therefore as if we were separated from our etheric body by an abyss filled, as it were, with ether, with universal cosmic ether, as if we were standing on the farther shore of our etheric body and that various activities were taking place there. Because we are here concerned with activities which all take place in time, we feel like a wanderer returning to our etheric body. In reality we are moving away from it more and more, but in clairvoyant consciousness we draw near to it. As we approach our etheric body we feel as if we were approaching something which repels us. We come as it were to a spiritual rock. Later we feel as if we were admitted into something. We were outside at first and then it seems as if we were admitted into something, as if we were now inside, but not in the same way as we had been within the etheric body in waking consciousness. Everything depends upon the fact that we are outside with our astral body and Ego and that we are only looking down into it – the etheric body, that is – that we are only inside our etheric body with our consciousness. And now we perceive what is happening there.

In a certain way, everything is transformed in the etheric body just as the physical body is transformed into the Paradise Garden. But what happens in the etheric body is much more intimately connected with the everyday processes taking place in man. Let us consider for a moment what sleep really means, what is the meaning of "being outside the etheric body and physical body". For we have assumed that the capacity for clairvoyance is awakened at this moment because man suddenly becomes clairvoyant during sleep or remains consciously clairvoyant at the moment of falling asleep. Let us consider what sleep is! The consciousness which permeates the physical and etheric bodies is now outside; within these bodies only vegetative processes now take place and all the forces used up during the day are replaced. We perceive how the forces, especially those used up in the brain, are renewed from out of the physical. Not that we would see the brain as the anatomist would see it, we see how the man of the physical world who serves as the instrument of our consciousness during waking life, we see how this man, forsaken by us as he is, is clearly demonstrating that he is our instrument, lies as it were *enchanted in a castle*.

Symbolised by the brain situated in the skull, terrestrial man appears like an enchanted being living in a castle. We see our human entity as a being imprisoned behind castle walls. The symbol of this, the shrunken symbol as it were, is our skull. Externally it appears in the form of a diminutive skull. But when we look at the etheric forces which fashion the skull then terrestrial man appears to us in fact as a being who, within the skull, finds himself imprisoned in this castle. And then from the rest of the organism there stream upwards the forces which sustain this being who is imprisoned in the skull as if in a fortified castle. The forces are directed upwards; first the force which comes from the instrument of the human astral body, an instrument which extends through the organism; everything that inspires man and lends him strength and energy streams through the nerve fibres. In terrestrial man all this is united and appears as the *mighty sword* which he has forged for himself on earth. Then the forces of the blood stream upwards; we gradually feel them, we come to recognise them, and they appear as that which in reality wounds the "brain" man lying in the enchanted castle of the skull. The forces which, in the etheric body, stream upwards towards the terrestrial man lying in the enchanted castle of the brain are like the *blood-stained lance*. And then we realise that we are able to observe everything that is permitted to stream towards the noblest part of the brain. Until now we did not have the slightest suspicion of this.

Thus you see that, from a different point of view, I come back to what I have already touched upon in these lectures. No matter how much animal flesh a man may eat, it is of no value for a certain part of his brain, it is simply ballast. Other organs may be nourished by it, but the etheric body of the brain immediately rejects all that comes from the animal kingdom. Indeed, from one part of the brain, from one small, important part of the brain, the etheric body rejects all that comes from the plant kingdom and tolerates only the mineral extract; there, in the vital part of the brain, it unites this mineral extract with the purest radiations entering through the sense organs. The purest element in light, sound, and warmth here comes in contact with the most refined products of the animal kingdom; the noblest part of the brain is nourished by this union of the most delicate sense impressions with the most refined animal products. The etheric body selects from the noblest part of the human brain all that comes from the plant and animal kingdoms. All the substances that man absorbs as food are directed towards the brain. But the brain has also less noble parts; these are nourished by everything that is carried up to the brain and which also provides sustenance for the whole organism. It is only the noblest part of the brain that must be nourished by the most perfect union of sensory perceptions and the finest mineral extract. We thus learn to recognise a wonderful cosmic relationship between man and the rest of the cosmos. We here perceive, as it were, a region where we are shown how human thought, through the instrument of the nervous system in the service of the astral body, forges the sword which lends man strength on earth; there we become acquainted with all that is mingled with the blood and which, to a certain extent, contributes to the death of all that is most noble in the brain. And this noblest element in the brain is continually sustained by the union of the most delicate sense perceptions with the purest products of the mineral kingdom. And then, during sleep, when thought is not using the brain, there stream towards the brain the products which have been formed in the lower organs of man from the plant and animal kingdoms.

Thus, when we penetrate into our own etheric body, it seems as if we have reached an abyss, and beyond it can see what is going on in the etheric body; and all this appears in mighty pictures representing the processes of the spiritual man during sleep. The Ego and the astral body – the spiritual man – descend into the castle which is simply a symbolic representation of what takes place in the skull where, wounded by the Lucifer forces in the blood, the human being lies asleep, he whose countenance betrays that his strength lies in thinking – that which must open itself to be nourished by everything that originates in the kingdoms of nature, that which in its noblest part must be served by all that is most refined which we have described before – all this represented symbolically was the origin of the Grail legend. And the legend of the Holy Grail tells us of that miraculous food, prepared from the finest activities of the sense-impressions and the finest activities of the mineral extracts, whose purpose is to nourish the noblest part of man throughout his life on earth; for all other nourishment would kill him. It is this celestial food which the vessel of the Holy Grail contains.

And what otherwise takes place, what thrusts its way up from the other kingdoms we find unobtrusively depicted in the original Grail legend where a meal is described at which a haunch of venison is first served up. This invasion of the brain where forever floats the Grail – the vessel destined for the noblest nourishment of the human, who here lies in the castle of the brain and who is killed by every other form of nourishment – all this is depicted. And the best account is not that of Wolfram, but the account where it is presented externally, exoterically – for almost everyone, when his attention is drawn to it, can recognise that the legend of the Grail is an occult experience which everyone can experience every evening. The best account, despite a certain profanation, is that of Chrestien de Troyes. And though he has given many indications of what we wished to convey, he has presented it in an exoteric form, for he refers to his teacher and friend who lived in Alsace and who supplied him with the esoteric teaching to which he gave an exoteric form. This took place in the epoch when it had become necessary to do this, on account of the transition of which I have spoken in my book *The Spiritual Guidance of Man*. It was shortly before this period of transition that the Grail legend appeared in exoteric form – in the year 1180.

Ideas of this nature still seem to be pure fantasy in the eyes of the world today because, in many cases, reality is attributed only to what is outside man. Man recognises himself to be the crown of creation in a much higher sense when he sees his physical body in its original grandeur, when he sees his etheric body working inwardly upon his physical body in order to reawaken to life what has been maimed and killed by that "sting" which, I said, had come from the blood. The etheric body works upon the physical body in order to reawaken it to life as far as possible; the etheric body sustains the physical body throughout its human life although it is already condemned to death at birth. The etheric body sustains it by expelling from a small part of the human organism all that comes from the animal and plant kingdoms, retaining only the most refined mineral extract, and uniting it with the purest impressions of the external sensible world. If we feel this really deeply enough, this noblest part of the human organism in each of us is revealed as a reproduction of the Holy Grail. I wanted to show you today by means of these two indications, how typical Imaginations appear, how, to authentic clairvoyance, the vision of the physical body is gradually transformed into Imaginations. And the Imagination of Paradise and the Imagination of the Grail belong to the most sublime Imaginations which man can experience, at least in this Earth cycle.

LECTURE SEVEN

The Hague, 26 March 1913

In the last lecture I tried to draw your attention to two legends, the Paradise legend and the Grail legend, in order to show that these two legends represent occult Imaginations which may really be experienced when the opportune moment arrives. When man, independent of his physical and etheric bodies, as he is in the unconscious condition of sleep, consciously perceives through clairvoyance his physical body and allows his perceptions to be inspired by the physical body, then he experiences the legend of Paradise; when he is inspired by his etheric body he experiences the legend of the Grail. Now it must be remembered that such legends were presented in the form of poetical inventions or religious legends and were accessible to mankind at a particular epoch and in a definite way. The original source of these legends that have been transmitted in the form of romances or religious writings in the course of the historical evolution of mankind is to be found in the Mysteries where their content had first been established by means of clairvoyant observation. And in the composition of these legends it was most important to ensure that both subject matter and tone were appropriate to the period and the people to whom they were given.

In the previous lectures we have shown how, through occult or esoteric development, the neophyte undergoes certain modifications in his physical and etheric bodies, We shall first have to consider the astral body and the Ego in greater detail, and then return briefly to the physical and etheric bodies. We saw that when man pursues his self-development in order to progress further through the acquisition of wisdom and truth, he thereby provokes modifications in the members of his spiritual and physical organisation. From the information derived from the Akashic Record of the widely different periods of evolution, we know that in the course of ordinary historical evolution these various members of human nature undergo modification, quite naturally, as it were.

We know that in the ancient Indian epoch, the first cultural epoch following upon the great Atlantean catastrophe, the processes of the etheric body of man were emphasised; that in the ancient Persian epoch the modifications of the astral body, in the Egypto-Chaldaean epoch the modifications of the sentient soul, in the Graeco-Latin epoch those of the intellectual or mind soul were stressed. And today the modifications of the consciousness soul are of primary importance. Now if in a certain epoch – in an epoch, let us say, in which the intellectual or mind soul undergoes a special modification, when the experiences within this soul are particularly important – if in this epoch a legend is given, it is important that it should be presented in such a way as to place special emphasis upon the peculiarities of this epoch, and that in the Mystery Centres from which those legends originated, the adepts should remind themselves that the legend must be of such a nature that the modifications taking place in the epoch of the intellectual or mind soul should be protected during that age against the possible harmful influences of the legend in question and should be specially adapted to the favourable influences of this legend.

The adept of the Mystery School whose duty it is to impart this legend to the world must not follow his innermost impulse alone; he must follow what the age dictates. If we undertake the relevant enquiries in this direction we shall understand better the modifications that occur, especially in the human astral body, when man undergoes occult-esoteric development.

In the case of the disciple of esotericism or in the person who seriously pursues an anthroposophical development, who makes spiritual knowledge the centre of his life, this astral body is isolated. In the case of the ordinary human being it is not so free, so independent as in the man who is in process of development; in the latter the astral body becomes to some extent independent, detaches itself, it does not slip unconsciously into a kind of sleep condition, but becomes autonomous and detached; it undergoes in a different way what the individual normally experiences in sleep. Thus the astral body attains a condition appropriate to it. In the ordinary man who lives in the exoteric world, the astral body is connected with the other bodies and each exercises its particular influence upon it. The single outstanding characteristic of this member does not then enter into consideration. When the astral body is insulated from the others its peculiarities are accentuated. And what are these peculiarities?

Now I have already indicated, perhaps to the horror of many members of the audience here, the characteristic feature of the human astral body on earth, namely, egoism. When the astral body, apart from the influences originating in the other vehicles, reveals its essential character, then this is seen to be egoism, the tendency to live exclusively in itself and for itself. That is the nature of the astral body. And for the astral body as such it would be disastrous, it would be a failing if it could not permeate itself with the force of egoism, if it could not say to itself: fundamentally whatsoever I do, I will achieve by my own efforts; I will owe it to myself and in all things will think solely of myself. That is the right temper of the astral body and if we bear this in mind we shall understand that esoteric development may be the source of certain dangers in this direction. Since esoteric development must of necessity liberate the astral body to some extent, those people who take up Anthroposophy half heartedly, without taking into consideration what true Anthroposophy seeks to offer, may, in the course of their esoteric training, emphasise this characteristic of the astral body, namely egoism. This can be observed in many theosophical and occult societies: whilst selflessness and charity to all as a moral principle are continually advocated, egoism flourishes on account of the natural dissociation of the astral body. For the detached observer this attitude is perfectly justified, but on the other hand it is rather disquieting when, in the name of a principle often invoked (note that I do not say, in the name of a principle too often invoked), we speak of charity to all, for under certain conditions of the soul life a person speaks most readily and most frequently of what he least possesses, of what he most lacks, and we can often observe that the greatest emphasis is laid upon principles precisely where they are most lacking.

Love for all one's fellow men ought in any event to be something that possesses the soul in the course of the development of mankind; it ought to inhabit the soul as something which is self-evident and which awakens the feeling: I must not speak of it so often in vain, I must not have it unnecessarily on my lips. Just as the well-known commandment says: Thou shalt not take the name of the Lord thy God in vain . . . so a commandment of truest genuine humanity might well be: Thou shalt not remind mankind so often and in vain of the obligation to love all one's fellow men, which must become the essential principle of thy soul. For if silence on many things is better than endless talk, then in this matter silence and quiet cultivation in the heart are far better means of developing brotherly love than talking about it too often.

Now the advocacy of this exoteric principle is in no way connected with what has just been described as the fundamental characteristic of the astral body – egoism, the attempt to be self-sufficient, self-possessed, self-reliant. And the question arises: How is it then possible to see aright this characteristic of the astral body which appears to us – let us not hesitate to use the expression – so odious at first, namely, the wish to be an absolute egotist? Let us start first of all from the simple facts of life.

There are cases in ordinary life in which egoism expands and where we must look upon this increase in egoism as a necessary factor in life. Consider for example the fundamental characteristic of maternal love and try to understand how in this case egoism extends from the mother to the child. The more we are familiar with the less educated section of the population and observe the leonine way, one might say, in which mothers defend their children, the more we notice that the mother regards an attack upon her child as an attack upon herself. Her child is an extension of her self; she would feel an attack upon her child as an attack upon herself. What she feels in her self she transfers to her child and it is a fortunate provision of nature that egoism can be transferred in this way from one person to another, that one person can regard his neighbour as part of himself, as it were, and is able therefore to extend his egoism to the other. Thus we see that egoism loses its negative aspects when a person, as he develops, transfers his feeling and thinking to another and considers his neighbour as part of himself. By extending their egoism to the child, mothers claim the child as their property; they count it as part of themselves and behave after the fashion of the astral body saying: Everything that is connected with me, lives through me, is part of me and so on. . . .

We can see something similar even in more trivial cases than maternal love. Let us assume that a man has a house, farm and land which he cultivates; let us suppose that – a whim of his perhaps – he loves his house, farm, land and farm workers as his own body; he sees them as an extension of his body and loves them as many a woman under certain circumstances loves her dress, as if it were part of her own body. In the case of the farmer in question his being expands to embrace the environment and when his solicitude extends to his environment so that he watches over his possessions and resists any attack upon them as if it were an attack upon his own person, then the fact that this whole world is permeated with his egoism is extremely beneficial to it.

Under certain circumstances what is called love may be very egoistic. Observation of life will show that what is called love is often self-seeking. But an egoism extended beyond the person may also be very disinterested, that is, it may cherish what belongs to it and protect it with devotion. It is precisely from such examples as this that we learn that life cannot be circumscribed by abstract notions. We talk of egoism and altruism and can devise very beautiful theories with notions such as these. But facts destroy such systems, for when egoism so extends its interest to the environment that it considers it as part of itself and cherishes and fosters it, then egoism becomes selflessness. On the other hand, if altruism seeks to make the whole world happy by imposing its own preferences, its own thoughts and feelings at all costs, and acts on the principle "if you will not be my brother I will smash your skull in", then even altruism may become extremely egoistic. Reality which is concerned with facts and forces cannot be circumscribed by abstract notions, and a great deal of what resists the progress of mind arises from the belief of immature minds that reality in some way can be tailored to fit abstract notions.

The astral body therefore may be described as an egoist. Consequently every development that liberates the astral body must reckon with the fact that the interests of mankind will expand and become progressively wider. Indeed, if our astral body is to liberate itself from the other members of human nature in the right way, then its interest must embrace the whole earth and the whole of mankind on earth. The interests of mankind on earth must become our interests, our interest must cease to be associated in any way with what is personal. Everything that concerns mankind, not only in our present epoch, but whatsoever has befallen mankind at any time in the course of earth evolution, must arouse our deepest interest. We must be in a position to consider not only those who are related to us by ties of blood, not only what is connected with us such as our house, farm and land as an extension of ourselves, but we must make everything associated with the evolution of the earth our own affair.

When, in our astral body, we are interested in all terrestrial affairs, when all the affairs of the earth become our own concern, then we may entrust ourselves to the egoity of our astral body. But it is necessary that the interests of mankind should become our interest. Consider from this point of view the two legends of which I spoke in the last lecture. When they were imparted to mankind, they were given with the intention of raising man above his private and personal interests in order to devote himself to the general interests of mankind.

The Paradise legend brings man back to that initial stage of earth evolution when he has not yet entered upon his first incarnation and is about to do so, when Lucifer approaches him, when his whole development lies before him, when he can actually enter into all the interests of mankind. The greatest educative legend that raises the deepest problems of education and training is the Paradise legend, the story which raises man to the vision of all mankind, which imprints in every human heart an interest which can speak to every man. When the images of the Paradise legend, as we have tried to comprehend them, penetrate into the human soul, they have the effect of permeating the astral body; and under the influence of this human being who has extended his horizon to embrace the whole earth, the astral body may make everything that now enters its domain its own concern. It has reached the stage when it is able to consider the interests of the earth as its own. Try seriously and conscientiously to reflect upon the universal pedagogic power of this legend and the deep spiritual impulse behind it.

The same applies to the legend of the Grail. Whilst the Paradise legend is given, so to speak, for the benefit of terrestrial humanity in so far as the latter contemplates the origin, the starting point of earth evolution, whilst the Paradise legend is therefore given in order to enlarge man's horizon to embrace the whole of mankind, the Grail legend is given in order that it may penetrate into the inmost depths of the astral body, into the fundamental interest of the astral body because, if left to itself, it becomes an egoist and takes into consideration only its egoistic interests.

When it is a question of the interests of the astral body one can err in two directions only, that of Amfortas and, before Amfortas is fully redeemed, that of Parzival. The true development of man lies between these two in so far as his astral body is concerned. This astral body tries to develop within itself the forces of egoism. But if it introduces personal interests into this egoism it is undermined; whilst it ought to extend its interests to embrace the whole earth these interests are limited to the single, isolated personality. But that must not be, for if it happens, then through the influence of the personality whose Ego is expressed in the blood, the whole human personality is wounded: we fall into the error of Amfortas. The fundamental error of Amfortas is to have introduced the personal wishes and desires, that may still persist in man, into the sphere where the astral body ought to have acquired the right to be an egoist. The moment we introduce personal interests into the sphere where the astral body ought to overcome personal interests, it is fatal, we become the wounded Amfortas.

But this other error may also lead to disaster that is only avoided if the being who is exposed to this misfortune is spotless like Parzival. Parzival sees the Grail pass repeatedly before him. To a certain extent he makes a mistake. Every time the Grail is carried past, it is on the tip of his tongue to ask for whom this food is really intended; but the question dies on his lips and finally the meal ends without his having asked the question. That is why he has to withdraw after the meal without having had the opportunity to repair his omission. It is as if a man, not yet fully mature, were to become clairvoyant for a moment during the night, as if he had been separated by an abyss from what is contained in the citadel of the body and were to contemplate it briefly – without having acquired the necessary knowledge, that is without having asked the appropriate question – as if everything were again withdrawn from his gaze; even if he were then to awake, he would not be able to enter into the citadel again. What did Parzival really fail to do?

We have heard what the Holy Grail contains. It contains that by which the physical instrument of man on earth must be nourished, that is, the pure mineral extract derived from all the foods and which unites in the purest part of the human brain with the finest sense impressions. To whom shall this food be served? As we discover when from the exoteric description we turn to the esoteric presentation in the Mysteries, it is destined for the human being who has acquired an understanding of what makes man sufficiently mature gradually to raise himself consciously to the vision of the Holy Grail. How does one attain the capacity to lift oneself consciously to the Holy Grail?

In the poem it is clearly indicated for whom the Holy Grail is destined. When we turn to the presentation of the legend of the Grail in the Mysteries, then it is abundantly evident. In the original legend the lord of the castle is the Fisher King, a King who ruled over a fisher folk. There was another who also dwelt amongst the fisher folk and who did not wish to be King over them, but desired a different relationship to these fishermen. He refused to rule over them as a King; he brought them something other than the reigning King – and this was Christ Jesus. An indication is thus given that the error of the Fisher King – who is Amfortas in the original legend – is the error which inclines him in the one direction. He is not wholly worthy to receive healing through the Grail because he wishes to rule over his fisher folk by force. He does not permit the spirit alone to rule amongst this fisher folk.

At first Parzival is not sufficiently awake inwardly to ask in full self-consciousness the question: What is the purpose of the Grail? What does it demand? It demands of the Fisher King that he should eradicate his personal interest and enlarge his interest to embrace the interest of all mankind after the fashion of Christ Jesus. In the case of Parzival it is necessary that he should raise his interest above that of a mere innocent spectator of things to the inner understanding of what is common to all men, of what is everyone's due – the gift of the Holy Grail. Thus, in a wonderful way, the ideal of the Mystery of Golgotha manifests itself between Parzival and Amfortas, the original Fisher King. At the decisive place in the legend there is a delicate hint that, on the one hand, the Fisher King has introduced too much personality into the spheres of the astral body, and that, on the other hand, Parzival has shown too little interest in the general affairs of the world; he is still too naïve, too unresponsive to world affairs. The immense pedagogic value of the Grail legend is that it could so influence the souls of the disciples of the Holy Grail that one perceived a kind of balance: on the one hand what Amfortas represented, on the other hand what Parzival represented. And they knew that a balance had to be established. If the astral body follows its innate, original interest it will raise itself to the ideal of universal humanity which is attained when these words become truth: For where two or three are gathered together in my name, there am I in the midst of them; no matter where these two may be found in the course of terrestrial evolution.

At this point I beg you not to mistake a part for the whole, but to take today's lecture and that of tomorrow together, for taken by itself a single lecture may cause misunderstanding. It is absolutely necessary that at this point the astral body of man should in its development be raised to the plane of humanity in a very special way so that the interests common to all mankind can become its interests, so that it feels hurt, affronted and sad at heart when mankind is offended in any way. Furthermore, when through his esoteric development man has gradually succeeded in making his astral body free and independent of the members of human nature, it is necessary that he should arm and protect himself first of all against possible influences of other astral bodies. For when the astral body becomes free, it is no longer protected by the physical and etheric bodies which are a strong citadel for the astral body. It is free, it becomes permeable and the forces in the other astral bodies could easily work into it. Astral bodies stronger than itself can gain influence over it unless it can arm itself with its own forces. It would be disastrous if someone were to be able to dispose freely of his astral body and yet in relation to the condition of his astral body were to remain as innocent as Parzival was initially. That will not do, for then all sorts of influences proceeding from other astral bodies might have a corresponding effect upon his astral body.

Now, in a certain respect, what we have just indicated may also be important in the external world. On earth men belong to different religious denominations; these denominations have their own cults and rituals. These rituals surround the believer with imaginations derived from the higher worlds with the help of the astral body. The moment such a religious community admits a man to its membership he is surrounded by imaginations which, whilst the rite is acting upon him, liberate his astral body. Any religious rite liberates the astral body to a certain extent, at least for a few brief moments. And the more powerful the rite the more it suppresses the influences of the etheric and physical bodies; the more it works by means of methods that liberate the astral body, the more is the astral body enticed out of the physical and etheric bodies during the ceremony in question. That is why – excuse the allusion, you might think that I am speaking derisively, but that is not my intention – there is no place so dangerous to sleep in as a church, because in sleep the astral body detaches itself from the etheric and physical bodies and also because what takes place in the rite takes possession of the astral body, for it is drawn down from the higher worlds with the help of other astral bodies. Thus the so called "dozing" in church, which is a very popular pastime in some areas, should be carefully avoided. This applies more to churches which practise a rite; it applies less to those religious communities who, because of their modernist outlook, have abandoned a particular cultus or limit themselves to a minimum of rites and observances. We are not speaking of these things from any preference or otherwise for a particular denomination, but purely in accordance with objective facts. When therefore the neophyte has liberated his astral body from his other vehicles, the impulses and forces acquired with the help of the other astral bodies easily exercise an influence upon him. It is possible therefore that a person who is able to dispose freely of his astral body, if he is stronger than another who is also able to liberate his astral body to some extent, may exercise a very powerful influence upon the latter. There is literally a transference of the forces of the astral body of the stronger personality to that of the weaker personality. If we then observe clairvoyantly the weaker personality, we find that his astral body bears within it the pictures and imaginations of the stronger astral personality.

You see how necessary it is that occultism, wherever it is to be cultivated, must be accompanied by morality; for clearly occultism cannot be cultivated unless we strive at the same time to emancipate the astral body from the other vehicles. The most disastrous thing in the field of occultism is when stronger personalities are animated by a thirst for power at all costs in order to further their personal interests, their personal aims and intentions. Only those persons who renounce completely all personal influence are really entitled to work in the field of occultism; the supreme ideal of the occultist who is to achieve anything legitimate is to sacrifice everything that is connected with his personality, and to eliminate as far as possible his personal sympathies and antipathies from whatsoever he wishes to achieve. He who has sympathies or antipathies for one thing or another and wishes to work as an occultist must carefully restrict his sympathies and antipathies to his private affairs and tolerate them only in this sphere. In any case he may not foster or cherish these sympathies and antipathies in a domain where it is intended that an occult movement should develop. And paradoxical as it may seem, we can state that to the occult master his teaching is a matter of little consequence; of least consequence is this teaching, which after all is circumscribed by the limitations of his talents and temperament. It will only be of consequence if nothing of a personal nature enters in, but solely what can be of help to the human soul. Therefore an occult teacher will never impose upon his age any aspect of his knowledge if he knows that it is unsuited to this age and might be suitable only for another age. We must bear these things in mind when we speak of the peculiar nature of the astral body under the influence of occult development.

In the preparation for our age and in the course of its further development a further complication arises. What is the characteristic of our epoch? It is the epoch of the development of the consciousness soul. Nothing is more closely connected with the egoism which is bound up with our narrow personal interests than the consciousness soul. Hence, in no other age has there been so great a temptation to confuse the most personal interests with the general interests of mankind. This epoch must gradually concentrate, as it were, the interests of mankind in the human Ego, especially that part of the human Ego which is the consciousness soul. We see in fact that as our age approaches, human interests are concentrated in the direction of the Ego, the central point of egoity. In this connection it is extremely instructive to ask oneself in all seriousness whether, for example, what St. Augustine wrote in his *Confessions* would ever have been possible in ancient Greece.

It would have been completely out of the question. By nature the inner being of the Greek was in harmony with the external world so that his external interests were at the same time his inner interests and the latter embraced the external world. Consider Greek culture in its entirety; it was of such a nature that we must presuppose a certain connection between the inner life of man and the external world. We can only understand Greek art, Greek tragedy, Greek historians and philosophers if we realise that in the Greeks the soul life still impregnated the external world and that the external world was as a matter of course conjoined with the inner life of the Greek people. Now compare this with the confessions of St. Augustine. For him everything is full of life, nothing is abstract; in his inner life he searches, digs, and explores. If we look for the personal individual note in the writings of St. Augustine we shall find it everywhere. Augustine lived long before the dawn of our epoch, but he prepared the ground for it. It is in his writings that we find the first dawn, long before the sunrise of the epoch which is wholly tailored to the development of the consciousness soul. This is evident in every line written by St. Augustine. And for those of more delicate sensitivity every line of St. Augustine can be distinguished from everything that was in keeping with the spirit of ancient Greece.

Now we know that Augustine anticipated the epoch in which selfhood, man's preoccupation with his own inner being within the physical body, is a characteristic of the age. We can then understand that a man like St. Augustine, who has wider interests and foresees the whole course of the development of mankind, is genuinely horrified when confronted by a human being who foreshadows a kind of egoism that must naturally follow from a certain higher development of the astral body. A pure, noble and great soul, the goal of Augustine is egoity. One might say that he selflessly attacks selfhood. He stands on the verge of the epoch when mankind has abandoned the wider interests of the external world. Remember that in the third post-Atlantean epoch every Egyptian directed his gaze to the world of stars and read his destiny there, and that the soul was still connected with interests common to all mankind. This was only possible of course when, thanks to the old instinctive clairvoyance, man was still capable of maintaining his astral body separate from his physical body. Therefore Augustine was horrified when confronted by a person who reminded him that higher development at first begets egoism! He can understand this, he feels it, and his instinct tells him that the age of egoity is approaching. When confronted by a person who represents a higher development beyond that of the physical body, he feels that this is an indication of egoism. He cannot understand that this person is transmitting at the same time an interest common to all mankind.

Try to enter into Augustine's feeling when, on his own admission, he faces the Manichaean Bishop Faustinus,[1] for it is he whom I have described. When confronted by Faustinus, Augustine experienced what a man may feel who awaits with mobility of soul the epoch of egoism and who wishes to protect this epoch against egoism by inner power alone; of necessity therefore he had to reject a man such as the Manichaean Bishop Faustinus. He rejected him because Faustinus in his eyes represented something that one should avoid, for he conceals within him something which the epoch of egoism will never understand in exoteric life. Thus the Manichaean Bishop Faustinus confronts the Church Father Augustine. Augustine, who foreshadows the epoch of the consciousness soul, comes face to face with a human being who preserves his connection with the spiritual world in so far as it can be preserved in a world occult movement and who thereby preserves the fundamental characteristic of the astral body which horrified Augustine, and rightly so from his point of view.

Let us move forward a few centuries. We now meet with a man at the university of Paris who is little known in the field of literature, for what he has written gives no idea of his personality. His writings appear pedantic but his personal influence must have been considerable; he seems to have been responsible in particular for a renewal of the Greek outlook on life in his circle. He was a typical renaissance man. He died in 1518 and up to the time of his death he taught at the university of Paris. This personality bore the same relation to the Greek world – though in a more exoteric way – as the Manichaean Bishop Faustinus to Manichaeism which, alongside many other things, had adopted especially in its traditions all the positive and negative aspects of the Egypto-Chaldaean epoch, the third post-Atlantean epoch.

Thus there was this Manichaean Bishop Faustinus whom we meet in connection with Augustine and who, because he is a Manichaean, has preserved the occult foundations of the third post-Atlantean epoch. In 1518 there died in Paris a man who had brought over, though exoterically, certain fundamental aspects of the fourth post-Atlantean age. Consequently to those of his circle who still worked in the field of traditional Christianity he was a sinister figure. The monks looked upon him as their arch-enemy; but he made a great impression on Erasmus of Rotterdam when the latter was in Paris. But to Erasmus it seemed that the external environment was ill-suited to what really dwelt in this remarkable soul. And when Erasmus had left for England he wrote to this man, who meanwhile had become his friend, that he wished he could rid himself of his gout-ridden body and fly through the air to England where he would find a more favourable soil for what dwelt in his soul. That this personality, who was active at that time, had been able to revive so vividly Greek feeling and Greek thinking we can best understand if we bear in mind the relationship between the sensitive Erasmus and this personality. Thus this personality who died in Paris in 1518 lived, one might say, precisely at the birth of the age of egohood. He lived as an enemy of those who wished to adapt the life of human souls to the age of selfhood and who felt a kind of horror in the presence of this soul who could act in this way because he wished to revive the Greek epoch, when man was closer to the egoity of the astral body. Erasmus felt an affinity with this personality who was called Faustus Andrelinus.

In the sixteenth century we meet with another personality in Central Europe who is described as a kind of wandering minstrel. The *Volksbuch* of the time relates that he abandoned traditional theology and subsequently refused to call himself a theologian. He preferred to call himself a man of the world and a physician. He laid the Bible aside for a time and devoted himself to the study of nature. Now in the age of transition from the ancient to the modern outlook the study of nature awakened in man, like Manichaeism and the ancient Greek culture, an understanding of astral egoity. Thus astral egohood brought a knowledge of what, at that time, stood on the boundary between alchemy and modern chemistry, between ancient astronomy and modern astronomy. This strange hesitation on the part of natural science between the old and the new outlook awakened in man – when he had laid his Bible aside for a time – such an astral activity that he had to come to terms with the question of egohood. Small wonder that those who with their traditions wished to come to terms with the epoch of egohood when the consciousness soul had established itself were horrified. And there arose in Central Europe the legend of the third Faust, Johannes Faust, also called Georgius Faust, who was an actual historical personality. And the sixteenth century welded together all the fears of the egoity of the astral body by combining the three Fausts, the Faustus of Augustine, the Faust of Erasmus and the Faust of Central Europe into a single figure, the figure of the *Volksbuch* of Central Europe who also became the Faustus of Marlowe. Goethe created his Faust by completely transforming the Faust of the popular legend. Through his Faust he wished to show that it is possible not to be afraid of this figure who bears within him that which awakens in us an understanding of astrality, but to understand him better, so that he can bring evidence of development and we can then say: We can redeem him. Whole epochs have grappled with the question of the egoistic nature of the astral body and in poetry and romances, even in history, we hear the echo of man's horror of the egoity of the astral body and his longing to solve this problem of the astral body in the right way, in a way that accords with the wise direction of the world and the esoteric development of the individual human soul.

LECTURE EIGHT

The Hague, 27 March 1913

When we touch upon the processes in the astral body and the Self of man as experienced in spiritual development it becomes increasingly difficult to describe them. For what we experience in these members is far removed from the experiences of daily life. In the ordinary life of the soul we feel life in the astral body, of course, as the ebb and flow of passions, emotions, impulses, desires and so on; we also feel as our inner life that which is expressed collectively in the Ego. But what is thus experienced is simply the reflection of the Self and the astral body in the etheric and physical bodies; it is not a conscious experience of the astral body and the Self. Through what we experience in the ordinary life of the soul we cannot have any precise idea of the actual experience we undergo in our astral body in the higher worlds. We must have recourse to a kind of representation appropriate to the higher worlds, we must have recourse to Imaginations and these Imaginations are actually experienced. But you must not imagine that the perception of these clairvoyant Imaginations is the only experience we have; to some extent it is not even the most important experience. It is what we experience inwardly that is of primary importance, the processes and inner trials that the soul undergoes when confronted by these Imaginations.

And this applies especially to that important and powerful Imagination such as the one which has been described in the Paradise Imagination. He who really experiences this Paradise Imagination, he who can hold it before him as a reality, as a conquest of the higher experience, feels himself caught up in an inner tumult of the soul, gripped by an inner psychic uncertainty and feels that he may err in either of the two directions described in the last lecture. On the one hand he feels himself powerfully attracted by all the passions and emotions which are the after-effect of the personal life which we live on the physical plane, for like myriad forces of magnetic attraction the personal interests which we have gradually developed in the physical plane work with ever increasing power. On the other hand, however, we feel something else. The nearer we approach the Paradise Imagination the more clearly we perceive it and the more powerful is the pull of these forces in the direction of personal interests, and their effect is to efface more and more this Paradise Imagination, or rather, they do not allow it to reveal itself in the right way; we become seemingly stultified. The personal interests, the emotions, feelings, impressions and so on, that we harbour in us are likewise myriads of magnetic forces which also act as opiates. And when we endeavour to reach the stage in our self-education when we actually observe the astral body more and more – when this Paradise Imagination is experienced outside our physical and etheric bodies, that is, in the astral body and Ego – when we have grasped the nature and true character of the astral body, then we know it to be an egoist. And at this stage of self-training this is only justified if we do not make the personal element, which shows itself in the myriad forces, the keynote of our egoistic interests, but make the interests common to mankind and the world more and more our own. At this stage of occult development we feel as a counterpoise to the egoism of the astral body something else that progressively asserts itself, the more the egoistic forces are active in the astral body which has now been set free. We have a sense of increasing solitude, of icy solitude. This glacial solitude is also part of what we experienced in this inner psychic tumult and it is this glacial solitude which saves us from excessive egoism; we have trained ourselves aright if at this stage of our occult development we can feel the impulse to be self-sufficient and self-contained, but at the same time can also feel the frosty solitude approaching us.

It is equally important to feel that we are gradually

LECTURE EIGHT

approaching the Paradise Imagination. When these two forces, the egoism which extends to world interests and the frosty solitude cooperate, then we draw ever nearer to the experience of the Paradise Imagination. And when this Imagination is present in its living reality, then the time has also come when we experience in the right way the meeting with the Guardian of the Threshold.[1] It is difficult to characterise in a nutshell the Guardian of the Threshold – I have already done so on several occasions in our anthroposophical lectures. Our task today is not so much to describe this Guardian of the Threshold as to describe the inward experiences in the human Self and its sheaths. If, as we visualise the Paradise Imagination, it becomes more and more vivid, and if we then meet the Guardian of the Threshold, we then feel the powerful influence of the magnetic forces already described, and as we confront the Guardian of the Threshold we feel – and this is a truly shattering experience – as if captivated, bewitched. For all these magnetic forces which limit us to our personal interests now exercise their strongest influence, and only when we have progressed sufficiently, when we have learned from this icy solitude that we are able to make the world's interest our own, do we pass the Guardian of the Threshold. We can then feel what may be called the union with the Paradise Imagination; we become one with it. We feel ourselves to be within it and this experience is like a feeling of justification in relation to interests of the world and we can now admit to ourselves: Yes, you may pursue your own interests, for they are now the interests of all mankind. But if we do not pass the Guardian of the Threshold, if we have not yet acquired sufficient universal interests, then personal interests claim our attention and there arises what is called in occultism: the failure to pass the Guardian of the Threshold. These personal interests obscure the Paradise Imagination and we then glimpse, as it were, only isolated fragments of it, vague imperfect impressions, and we feel that we are dragged back again into our personal life. But the case may arise that we have been granted, to a certain extent, the possibility of having clairvoyant experiences, but these experiences are really *maya* experiences which may be quite misleading, for they are at all times permeated with, or clouded by personal interests.

Through such an experience we can fully understand, and we now take the matter seriously, that personal interests must be transformed into world interests if we wish to see the true reality of the spiritual world. Before reaching this stage of development we cannot really believe this, since personal interests militate against this belief; but at the moment we meet the Guardian of the Threshold we are aware of this need to transform our personal interests.

We have now reached a very hazardous stage in the description of occult conditions. Nevertheless, we shall attempt to indicate the next steps as they appear from occult experience and in the way in which they must be presented if we are to take into account the fact that those listening are trying, in a certain sense, to develop these things in themselves and to work upon them further. These things can be clothed in abstract ideas; we must attempt to recapture what is revealed to clairvoyant vision. Now one must not imagine that this clairvoyant vision can be depicted schematically within a fixed framework. What I propose to describe is again a typical experience like that of the Paradise experience; we must really have passed through this experience in order to discover what knowledge and spiritual vision really are. Before this we can have no real idea, no actual experience of spiritual vision. But when an experience of this kind is described, we can understand it if we apply sound common sense. However, it must now be described as it appears to clairvoyant vision.

Let us assume that the neophyte has passed the Guardian of the Threshold, has celebrated his meeting with the Paradise Imagination and felt himself so completely at one with it that this Paradise Imagination has now become his own greater astral sheath. He can still feel his own astral body and knows that it is connected with his Ego, but he knows at the same time that this new astral body extends its interests to everything that concerns the entities and Beings of the Paradise Imagination. When he has achieved his union with the Paradise Imagination he may have the following impression: He will perceive his own astral body as a part of himself, and when he has experienced in adequate measure what has been described as icy solitude, then this feeling will become a force within him and will preserve him from contemplating only himself when he has realised his union with the Paradise Imagination. He will thereby create for himself the necessary organ to perceive other entities. His occult vision will first fall upon another Being, a Being who will make a special impression upon him because he will appear like himself. He himself feels that he is in his Self and in his astral body; the other Being will also appear to him at first with a Self and an astral body. The reason for this is that the characteristics and powers which a person brings with him for this moment of meeting the Guardian enable him to perceive just such a Being that manifests itself as a Self and an astral body. The neophyte will now have the following experience – and it will be evoked by the frosty solitude which he has learned to bear:

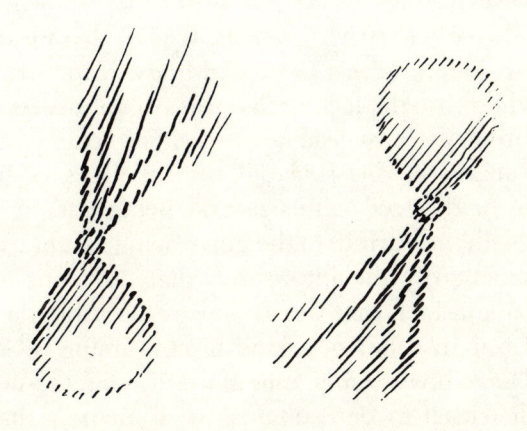

His astral body with its energies will give the impression of wanting to strive in an upward direction. If I were to represent this diagrammatically I should have to draw it in the following way – but, as I have said, this is only a schematic rendering. I draw the Self as the nucleus of a comet and the astral body as the tail of the comet shooting upwards and outwards; but as I said, this is only a schematic representation, for the neophyte really sees a Being, sees himself as a Being and this vision is much more complex than the perception of his own Being in a physical form. He also sees the other Being within his own Self. As I have said, that is a typical experience; it simply means that the clairvoyant's eye falls at first upon this Being, but he feels that this Being is not in a sphere of icy solitude as he is himself, and consequently its astral body seems to be directed downwards. It is most important to experience this, to feel oneself as if in an astral body which opens upwards, which directs its streams of astral energy upwards, wishes to stream upwards and to see the other Being as a Self whose astral body directs its forces in a downward direction.

Now there arises in the consciousness of Self in relation to this typical experience something like the following: You are inferior, you are of less value than this other Being. What is valuable in this other Being is that it can open its astral body downwards, can, as it were, pour its forces downwards. And we receive the impression that we have left the physical world, whilst the forces of the astral body of the other Being are directed downwards, towards the physical world and work there as forces of benediction; in brief, we have the impression that we are confronted by a Being which may send down to earth as a beneficent rain what it has acquired in the spiritual world, that we ourselves cannot direct our astral body downwards; the astral body seeks to strive upwards. We feel that we are inferior because we cannot direct our astral body downwards. And we have furthermore the feeling that this consciousness which has arisen within us must lead to a spiritual activity. A spiritual decision matures; this spiritual resolve urges us to lay our loneliness at the feet of this second Being and to warm our coldness with the warmth of the other Being, to unite with it. We have momentarily the impression that our consciousness is being extinguished, that we are now responsible for a kind of death of our own Being, a kind of consuming by fire of our Being. There now flashes into the self-consciousness, which already felt itself to be extinguished, something that we now become aware of for the first time – Inspiration. We feel ourselves inspired. It is like a dialogue, a typical dialogue that is now exchanged with a Being whom we only come to know because he bestows his inspiration upon us. If we are really able to understand what this Being communicates as his voice of Inspiration, we might translate what he says approximately in the following words: "Because you have found the way to the other and have united yourself with his bounteous sacrifice you may now return to earth with him, in him, and I will make you his guardian on earth." And we have the feeling that we have received something of infinite importance into our soul because we have been permitted to hear these words of Inspiration. In the spiritual world there is a Being of greater worth than ourselves, a Being who is permitted to send down his astrality as a benediction. That we may unite with him, that we may be his guardian when we have descended to earth with him, this experience teaches us to understand how, as physical beings on earth, we are really related with our physical and etheric sheaths to the higher forces that impregnate the Self and the astral body. With our physical and etheric sheaths we are guardians of that which is to develop further and further to higher spheres. And when we feel our external being as the guardian of our inner Being, this inner experience provides us with a true insight into the relationship between the external sheaths and the inner Being of man.

Now when we have passed the Guardian of the Threshold this experience I have just described is not an isolated experience, it is followed by another. First of all I have described the purely clairvoyant and inspired experience that we may have when, outside the physical and etheric bodies, we have succeeded in uniting with the Paradise Imagination and then have received that Inspiration which first gives us an idea of the relationship between the sheaths and the Self. Having passed the Guardian of the Threshold the second impression is added to the first; the eye is directed past the Guardian of the Threshold down to the physical world below. I indicate the boundary between the higher spiritual worlds and the physical world by a line; above is

120   THE EFFECTS OF SPIRITUAL DEVELOPMENT

the realm of the spiritual world and below that of the physical world.

We now look down into the physical world and there another image is revealed: the image of ourselves here below on earth. We perceive our own astral body, but this astral body, which now appears as if in a reflection, is directed downwards; it does not seek to direct its energies towards the spiritual world, it

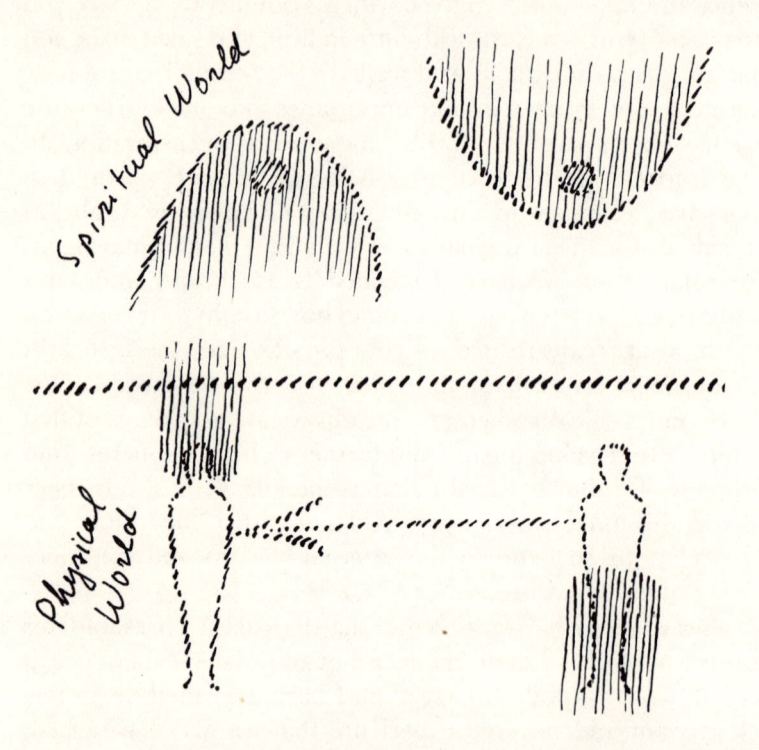

Spiritual World

Physical World

clings as it were to the physical plane and does not aspire to the heights. We also see the reflection of the other Being whose astral body streams upwards. We have the feeling that this astral body is streaming into the spiritual world. We see ourselves, and we see the other and we have the feeling: You find yourself in the physical world once more; in place of the other Being a quite different human Being is there, he is a better man than you; his astral body strives upward, it rises upward like smoke. Your astral body strives towards the earth; like trailing smoke, it tends earthwards. As we look down we have the feeling of a Self that dwells within us and we have this terrible impression: A determination is slowly maturing within you, a dreadful resolve, the determination to kill the other who is superior to yourself. We know that this decision does not come wholly from the Self, for the Self dwells in the spiritual world. It is another Being that speaks out of us here on earth and it is this Being who prompts us to kill the other. And now we hear again the voice which previously had inspired him, but now it is like a voice fraught with dire revenge and asks: "Where is thy brother?" And from this lower Self bursts forth the voice which answers the earlier voice. Previously the Inspiration was as follows: "Because you have united yourself with the beneficent powers of the other Being you will pour your beneficent powers earthwards and I will make you guardian of the other Being." Now from this Being which one recognizes as one's Self comes the retort: "I will not be my brother's keeper." First comes the determination to kill the other, then the protest against the voice which inspired him in the following way: "Because you wish to unite your coldness with the warmth of the other being I appoint you to be the guardian of the other." And then the protest "I will not be his keeper."

When we have had this Imaginative experience we know everything of which a human soul is capable and then we know one thing in particular: That the noblest virtues of the spiritual world when perverted to their opposite may have most destructive effects on the physical plane. We know that in the depths of the human soul, through the perversion of noblest readiness to sacrifice the Self, the wish may arise to kill one's neighbour. From this moment we know what is meant by the story of Cain and Abel in the Bible – but only from this moment – for the story of Cain and Abel is none other than the representation of an occult experience, indeed of the very one we have just described. If, for other reasons than those which once existed in the course of human evolution, the author of the story of Cain and Abel had been able to describe what had happened before the expulsion from Paradise, he would have described the first experience, indicated in the upper part of the diagram. But he begins with the story of Paradise and describes the reflected image; for what Cain felt towards Abel before the period of terrestrial evolution indicated by the story of Paradise is described above. And after the temptation and after the loss of vision which is regained through the Paradise Imagination, Cain's readiness to sacrifice the Self had changed into the desire to kill the other, which had now become a reality on earth. And the cry recorded in the Bible: "Am I then to be my brother's keeper?" is the reply to the other Inspiration: "I will appoint you here on earth to be the guardian of the other."

From this description you will understand that these typical experiences are certainly important, for they establish a certain union between what may be today and the interests most common to all mankind. But at the same time they show us very clearly that, in what we experience in them in the ebb and flow of the soul life, the main thing is to feel how the evolution of mankind has made this colossal leap forward from what I described to you as the first pre-terrestrial Imagination to that which is presented in the story of Cain and Abel as an event in human evolution after the expulsion from Paradise, after that expulsion through which the Guardian of the Threshold has become invisible to man. It is the awareness of this leap forward in the evolution of mankind that first really shows us what this terrestrial man is; for when we feel profoundly what has just been described, we gradually realise that this terrestrial man as we know him today is a perversion of what he was in ancient times. And we know for certain what would have become of us if nothing else had intervened. If we had simply developed in this terrestrial evolution without interference, we should have known of what this story of Cain and Abel is the reflection here on earth. And this we were not allowed to know at first.

It is only in our present epoch that man is permitted to know that the story of Cain and Abel is the reflection of a great sacrifice. Everything that was in the spiritual world, which existed before the Fall, was veiled; the Guardian himself

LECTURE EIGHT

concealed it from us when, in other words, man was driven out of Paradise. And that could only happen because the physical and etheric bodies of man were now so permeated with forces that he no longer follows out the reflection, the intention of the spiritual world, for assuredly he would carry it out if he were to feel all that is in the astral body. The physical and etheric bodies stupefy man to such an extent that his wish to kill the other is not realised. Consider what this simple sentence means: Because the beneficent divine-spiritual powers gave man a physical body and an etheric body to prevent him from looking back, a kind of stupefaction as a consequence blanketed the desire to engage in the war of all against all. This desire is not active in the soul because the physical and etheric bodies of man have been prepared in such a way that this wish is stifled. A person cannot see his astral body and therefore this wish remains unknown to him, he does not carry it into effect. If we really wish to describe the interaction of the astral body and the self we must describe things which not only are concealed from human nature, but which of necessity must remain concealed. What then has happened as a result of this stifling of the desire to kill and similar wishes aiming at the destruction and annihilation of community life and other forms of corporate life on the physical plane? They have become weakened; the human soul feels them only in a weakened form, feels them only slightly. And the dim feeling of those wishes which would be something terrible if man were to grant them free scope, as they really are – that is the true human terrestrial knowledge.

I will now give you first of all the definition of what is meant by human earthly knowledge. It consists of the blunted impulses of destruction, of Shiva in his most terrifying aspect, but so blunted that he cannot express them to the full, but himself has become impoverished, has been reduced to the world of human ideas – this is the inner *maya*, the knowledge of man. This knowledge had to be weakened, and equally the impulses and inner forces, in order that the originally destructive element where Ahriman holds sway – for originally it was Ahriman who provoked this wish – in order that Ahriman's power should be so far emasculated that man should not fall victim to Ahriman and thereby make himself permanently a servant of Shiva. The totality of these forces had to be so far weakened that they only hold sway in man in so far as he can enter into the being of others with his ideas and conceptions. When we try to impose an idea upon another, when we try to implant in another a conception of our own, then this conception we have implanted into the other person is the blunted weapon of Cain which was plunged into Abel. And because this weapon was thus blunted it became possible for that which had suddenly been transformed into its opposite to pass over into evolution. And thus slowly instead of developing destructive impulses which he was not permitted to develop in the physical world, man underwent a gradual evolution through reinforcement of his knowledge – first he develops factual knowledge, then Imaginative knowledge which enters into the Being of the other, then Inspirational knowledge which penetrates more deeply into the Being of the other and finally Intuitive knowledge which enters wholly into the other and lives on spiritually in the other Being. Thus we gradually fight our way to an understanding of what this Self really is. In its innermost nature the astral body is a great egoist; the Self is more than a great egoist, it wishes to be not only a Self, it wants to be a Self in the other, to identify itself with the other. And the knowledge that has been acquired on earth is this weakened desire to enter into the other, to extend all that one is, not only in oneself, but beyond the Self into the other. It is the intensification of egoism beyond itself, beyond its narrow limitations.

If you bear in mind the origin of this knowledge you will then understand that there is always the possibility of misusing it, for if this knowledge is a true knowledge of the Self then the moment it goes astray it is immediately abused. It is only when we progress further, when we gain a more spiritual understanding of the other and when, by extending the horizon of the astral body to world interests, we succeed in renouncing all constraint over the other, when we leave him completely to himself and do not value his interests more highly than our own, only then do we become mature enough to rise to higher knowledge. We cannot recognise a Being of the Hierarchy of the Angels unless we have reached the stage when we are more interested in the inner Being of the Angels than in our own Being. As long as we are more interested in our own Being than that of the Angels, we cannot recognise them. We must first open ourselves to world interests, then to interests that go still further, so that we may attach greater importance to others than to ourselves. The moment we attempt to develop further in occult knowledge and yet set greater store on our Self than the other Beings whom we wish to know, in that moment we go astray. And if you follow this line of thought you arrive at a true picture of what black magic really is; for black magic begins where occult activity is practised openly without our being in a position to expand our own interests into world interests, without our being able to set greater store on other interests than on our own.

In reality we can only draw attention to these things in order to hint at the ideas, for they are too important to give more than a suggestion. I wanted to show how it is possible gradually to come to recognise the astral body and the Self that dwell within us in their true nature and not in *maya*; for what man experiences inwardly as his astral body is not the true astral body but only the reflection of the astral body in the etheric body. And what man calls his Self is not the real Ego, it is the reflection of the Ego in the physical body. A man only experiences reflections of his inner being. If he were to experience the configurations of his own astral body and Ego before he was sufficiently mature, then destructive impulses would arise in him, he would become an aggressive Being and he would be animated by the desire to do harm. And these things form the basis of black magic. Although the paths followed by black magic are very diverse, the result is always a kind of alliance with Ahriman, with Shiva. We only learn to know the astral body and the Ego in their true form if we acknowledge at the same time the necessity to develop them and to make them worthy of being what they are destined to be. The essential nature of the astral body is egoism; it must be our ideal to be allowed to be an egoist because the interests of the world become our interests; it must be our ideal to be allowed to enter into the other Being because it is our firm intention not to use the other as a means to our own ends, but to esteem him as more important than ourselves. Self-education must be sufficiently developed to feel this upper picture (see diagram, p. 120) in all its occult and moral significance; to transform gradually this picture which is ourselves so that our emotions, impulses, desires and passions can no longer be stirred, but that with our familiarity with the astral body we are at home in frosty solitude and thereby open ourselves to the warmth, to the warm interest which radiates from the other Beings, and we seek to unite with the beneficent forces proceeding from these other Beings. We are here shown at the same time the first step which enables us to lift ourselves gradually to the Higher Hierarchies in their true form. We do not attain to the Beings of the Higher Hierarchies if we are not worthy enough to face this Imagination and Inspiration which have already been described, and if we are not able to tolerate their counterpart, that is to say, the evil propensities hidden in the depths of human nature when it was cast down from the spiritual world into the physical world. If we do not wish to look upon the double image of Cain and Abel, namely, the lower Self and the image of our higher Self, which at the same time is the mediator between ourselves and the Higher Hierarchies, we cannot grow spiritually. But then when we are able to cultivate in ourselves the feeling indicated here, we experience our Self, and from the Self as our point of departure we gain access to the higher orders of the Hierarchies.

LECTURE NINE

The Hague, 28 March 1913

I used to know a poet[1] who died some years ago. In the late eighties of the last century he confided to me one day that he was very worried about the future. I can assure you that the way he expressed his anxiety was somewhat paradoxical, but there was no doubt that his anxiety was very real, especially in relation to the future trend he wished to indicate by his paradox – this anxiety in fact inclined him to a certain pessimism. In his opinion the future evolution of mankind would tend chiefly to the increasing development of the head and compared with the head the rest of man's organism would atrophy. He was in deadly earnest over this idea and expressed his fear in the following paradox: A time might come, he believed, when the rational, intellectual nature of man might take over control to such an extent that in the end the head would become a huge ball, and men would then roll like balls over the surface of the earth. His fears were very real; for he reflected that we are living in the epoch of intellectualism when the intellectual faculties, which are expressed in the head, are emphasised. He believed that these intellectual powers would progressively increase and that man was moving towards an unenviable future.

Now this is a very paradoxical way of voicing his fears and in a certain sense one might say that the anxiety which inspired his pessimism is also paradoxical. But as is so often the case, man's intellectual power has a tendency to exaggerate, to jump to conclusions when some observation or other is under consideration, and that is also the case here. There is ample evidence for this both in the external exoteric life and within the anthroposophical way of thinking. We need only look around a little and we shall find that the experiences, the actual observations which man has made over the centuries have always produced a crop of theories and hypotheses. How many hypotheses have been consigned to oblivion in the course of human evolution, how many have been shown to be worthless! In the anthroposophical and occult domain we often find that if someone who has undergone an occult training and therefore has to some extent acquired clairvoyant powers communicates certain facts from genuine clairvoyant observation, then along come the theorists and invent all kinds of schemes and plausible theories which are expanded and developed. Often the observation is trifling, but the schemes and theories built upon it make mountains out of mole hills. That is always the danger, for the intellect has this tendency to exaggerate out of all proportion. We find this tendency in a somewhat unobtrusive form in the well-known book *Esoteric Buddhism* by Sinnett. The book is based upon a number of genuine esoteric facts which occupy the central part of the book and refer to the middle period of the earth's evolution. On these facts the writer built a system of rounds and races which revolve and follow cyclically upon each other always more or less in the same way. They are inferences, theories elaborated from the few genuine data to be found in the book, data which accord with the facts. And this was also the case with the poet I have referred to. Deep down within him he had a kind of unconscious instinctive Imagination which told him something of the truth, an ounce of truth, one might say, which he multiplied a hundredfold. We often meet with cases such as this in the world. Now where does the truth lie?

The truth is this: In the present age, in our present earth cycle, man's head is undergoing a certain evolution and in the future the formation of the head, the whole structure of the head, will undergo further modifications. Looking ahead to a far-distant future of the earth we have to imagine that, for example, the structure of the human forehead, of the nose and jaws, will have undergone important modifications whilst, in a certain sense, the rest of the terrestrial organism of man will have retrogressed; but during the earth epoch, the relationship of the head, which is in process of development, to the rest of the body will of course never be that of a ball rolling away. This will be perceived only to a minute extent. In earlier epochs of earth evolution on the other hand, before the middle of the Atlantean epoch, the rest of the human organism was capable of change, was in process of transformation. Apart from the head the human organism has changed relatively little – I repeat *relatively* little – since the middle of the Atlantean epoch, whereas, before the Atlantean epoch, the rest of the human organism underwent considerable modifications. From this you will be able to draw the conclusion – correctly this time, since it is simply an observation clothed in words – that the further we go back into the Atlantean and Lemurian epochs the more different fundamentally man appears even to himself. In the ancient Lemurian epoch man looked totally different from the person he is today.

The vision man would have had of himself in the latter part of the Lemurian epoch is revealed to him to a certain extent when he gradually begins to receive that clairvoyant impression leading to what we have described as the Paradise Imagination. I have told you that this Paradise Imagination corresponds to a complete description of the human being, of the physical body, as Paradise itself. Man becomes dissociated, as it were, becomes a divided being; the present corporeal nature appeared diffused in the manner already described; but at the same time, the time to which we look back clairvoyantly when we see the Paradise Legend unrolling before us, a mighty leap forward was made. And through this sudden leap forward, which can also be observed by means of clairvoyance, what might be called the extension of the human entity was, relatively rapidly, compressed to the dimension which became the starting point of man's subsequent evolution. Nevertheless, immediately after the time corresponding to the Paradise Imagination, the form of man was very unlike that of today. And fundamentally, all that surrounded him in the kingdoms of nature was very different from what surrounds him in nature today.

In the previous lectures given here, I said that it was possible for the neophyte to attain to this Paradise Imagination if he were suddenly to become clairvoyant for a moment during sleep and to look back to his physical and etheric bodies and allow himself to be stimulated by them to experience this Paradise Imagination. In general it may be said that one must have made great strides in esoteric development if one wishes to attain to this Paradise Imagination. One must have won many victories over oneself, must have undergone many trials in order to transform one's personal interests into the interests common to all mankind and the world. When man passes from deepest sleep – for these are degrees of sleep – to a less deep sleep and in this higher sleep becomes clairvoyant, there is revealed what later in terrestrial evolution became reality – the condition of man in the ancient Lemurian epoch after having made the great leap forward. We can say therefore that it is possible to see this primordial period of the earth by isolating one's Self and one's astral body from the physical and etheric bodies and looking back at them. Now since nature's expedient comes to one's aid, for we are outside our physical body during the night, we can use this expedient and so regulate our training that, as if awakening out of sleep without re-entering the physical body, as if awakening in another state of consciousness, we see the physical body. From this you will be able to gather that this vision of which we have just spoken provides the only real possibility of knowing the form man had in the primeval past.

A time will come in the far distant future when we shall be aware of the following and will say: How extraordinary were those people of the nineteenth and twentieth centuries! They believed that by scientific research and from the study of the animal kingdom around them they could draw conclusions about the ancestry of man. Now the true development of human knowledge shows that we can only arrive at a real knowledge of the origin of man on earth, of his original form, through clairvoyant observation; that we can never gain insight into what man was like in the Lemurian epoch, for example, except through clairvoyance, through retrospective vision stimulated by the impressions furnished by our own physical and etheric bodies. Then it will be seen – and this will be confirmed in the future – that the form of man never had any affinity with the animal forms surrounding man in the nineteenth and twentieth centuries, for the forms of man in the Lemurian epoch, and which are revealed to his clairvoyant consciousness in the manner already indicated, differ from all the animal forms around man in the nineteenth century. And even the terms we have used, bull, lion, and so on, are only used by way of comparison. Men of the future will say that it is perfectly ridiculous to see how the people of the nineteenth and twentieth centuries traced back their origin to simian ancestry, for in the Lemurian epoch apes did not exist in the form in which they later appeared on earth; they only evolved at a much later period out of decadent and degenerate human forms.

It is only towards the middle of the Atlantean epoch that any trace of animal beings which may be compared to the apes of today is to be found by retrospective clairvoyant vision. The further we go back in the evolution of mankind, the more we perceive that, to the clairvoyant vision of our Self during sleep, in the night, our form, the structure of ancient times, has been preserved to some extent. Thus, when man surveys himself, he becomes aware of his physical body enclosed in an infinitely more delicate etheric body – the term etheric is not to be confused with our present ether. Thus man appeared to himself in a form more akin to a vivid dream picture than to the form of flesh and blood that we know today. We must become familiar with the idea that when the Self and the astral body are outside the human being they can scarcely see the head; it appears to be quite nebulous; it is not completely effaced, but appears to be quite vague and indefinite. On the other hand the rest of the organism seems more distinct. It is also nebulous, but gives the impression that the human being is not a being of flesh and blood, but is endowed with a more powerful organisation. Paradoxical as it may seem, it is nevertheless true that when a man perceives himself clairvoyantly in sleep, he sees his physical and etheric bodies at certain moments in a form that recalls that of the centaur! In the centaur the extension of the human aspect in the upper part which bears the human face is quite nebulous; the other part which does not bear any relation to any existing animal form, but which, in a certain respect, is reminiscent of animal forms, gives an impression of power, so that to the spiritual eye this part seems stronger, more solid than the present human form of flesh and blood.

I have already touched upon these questions in an earlier course of lectures,[1] but you must realise that all these Imaginations, except the Paradise Imagination, are transient and can be portrayed from different angles. I could equally well portray a somewhat different aspect – and you would see that this simply corresponds to another period of development – and then we should arrive at the form of the sphinx. The successive stages in the evolution of man are depicted from different points of view and from different angles. The mythological images, the so called mythological symbols, are far more true than the fantastic intellectual theories of modern scholarship.

Thus, during the night, the human figure assumes a very peculiar form. And something else now becomes clear. When we observe clairvoyantly this lower part of the centaur which recalls an animal entity, we discover something which makes a definite impression upon us. I said yesterday that these impressions, these inner experiences are really the vital factor, the essential element; the images are important, but the inner experiences are still more important. We receive a certain impression and we know subsequently: What impels me during the day towards purely personal interests, what implants in my soul purely personal interests, originates in what I observe during the night as the animal aspect of my form. During the day I am not aware of it; but it lives in me as a conflux of forces and these are the forces which drag me down and tempt me to succumb to personal interests. And when we develop this impression more and more we come to recognise the reality of Lucifer and the part he plays in our evolution. The further we look back clairvoyantly to the time that corresponds to the Paradise Imagination, the more beautiful becomes the structure which only at a later time really recalls our animal nature. And if, furthermore, we go back to the Paradise epoch when the animal nature of man appears as though detached from man himself and multiplied into bull, lion, eagle, we may then say that these forms which we designate by these names of ancient times, may also be for us, in a certain sense, symbols of beauty. These forms become more and more beautiful, and if we go still further back to the time which I spoke of yesterday, when we described the impression of the sacrifice, we arrive at the epoch when Lucifer's true form appears to us in sublime beauty, that form he wished to preserve during the evolution from the Old Moon to the Earth.

From the account I gave in *Occult Science* you know that the astral body was given to man on Old Moon, and that what we bear in our astral body played a great part on the Old Moon. We described it as selfhood, as egoism. This egoism had to be implanted in man on the Old Moon, and since man received his astral body on the Old Moon egoism has its seat in the astral body; and since Lucifer has preserved his Moon nature, he has brought egoism to the earth as the inner soul character of his beauty. On the one hand, therefore, he is the Spirit of beauty, and on the other hand, the Spirit of egoism. And what we may call his transgression is simply that he transplanted to the earth something which, if I may use the expression, was appropriate on the Old Moon, that is to say, the power to permeate, to impregnate himself with egoism. Thereby man has the possibility, as has often been said, of becoming in himself, in his inner being, a self-contained, free being, which he could never have become if Lucifer had not transplanted egoity from the Old Moon to the earth. Thus, in inner experience we come to know Lucifer as the nocturnal Spirit. And we owe it to that transformation, which our Self and astral body undergo in the course of occult development, that we feel ourselves during the night in the presence of Lucifer.

The idea that man, when he falls asleep and becomes clairvoyant, is aware that during the night he is in the presence of Lucifer, this idea you will perhaps find distasteful at first if you take a superficial view. But if you reflect more deeply, you will soon realise that it is more sensible to learn to recognise Lucifer, that it is better to *know* that we are in his presence, than to believe he is not there, whilst Luciferic forces are active within us unseen, for they are also active in us during the day. The worst of it is not that Lucifer is present, for we gradually come to recognise him as the Spirit who brings freedom; the worst of it is that we do not recognise him. But after men had caught sight of him, as it were, when he tempted them in the Lemurian epoch, they were not permitted to see him any more; for this original temptation was followed by innumerable lesser temptations. Therefore the divine spiritual Being charged with the progress of mankind had to throw a veil over the nocturnal vision. This entailed the loss of everything that man would otherwise have seen during sleep. Sleep veils in darkness the world which man inhabits from the time of falling asleep until the moment when he awakens. The moment the veil is lifted we would indeed find that Lucifer is at our side. If man were strong enough this would do no harm; but since, at first, in terms of terrestrial development, he could not be sufficiently strong, this veil had to be drawn over the time he spent in sleep at night. And after the original temptation, which resulted in the possibility of human freedom, other temptations arising from the direct vision of Lucifer from the moment of falling asleep until the moment of awakening should not be able to affect man.

Now there is a counterpoise to this. We cannot see Lucifer during the night unless we see his companion Ahriman during the day. And so for the person who has reached this point in the development of the Self and the astral body, the waking consciousness that gives rise to the perception of external objects is different from that of the ordinary man. He realises that he approaches things differently than he was accustomed to do before the development of his Self and the astral body. He first learns to look upon certain impressions which he formerly accepted in an abstract way as the activities of Ahrimanic beings. Thus he learns to recognise that desire – not that which springs from within, for that is Luciferic, but that which comes from without, which excites desire in man from without – which attracts him to the objects and beings around, so that he follows this attraction from personal motives. In short, everything from without that tempts us to indulgence, this we recognise as the mark of Ahriman. We learn to recognise as the hall-mark of Ahriman everything from without that inspires fear in us. The two poles are enjoyment and fear. Around us are the so-called material world and the so-called spiritual world; both these worlds appear to waking consciousness as *maya* or illusion. The sensible world appears as *maya*, for people do not realise that wherever external objects and entities stimulate the pleasures of the senses Ahriman is lurking, and it is he who excites desires in the soul. The fact that everywhere matter is imbued with spirit – which materialists deny – engenders fear; and when the materialists perceive that fear is welling up from within, from the astral domain, they stupefy themselves by inventing materialistic theories. And the words of the poet are profoundly true: "The naïve never notice the devil, that is Ahriman, even when he has them by the throat." What is the purpose of monistic meetings? To conjure up the devil. This is literally true, but people do not know it. Whenever meetings of materialistic monists are held today, proclaiming in neatly rounded theories that matter alone exists, Ahriman has them by the throat. There is no better opportunity for studying the devil today than to attend the gatherings of materialists or monists. Thus when a man has undergone a certain development in his astral body and Self, Ahriman accompanies him at every step. When we begin to see him, we can protect ourselves against him, for we are aware that behind the allurements of sensual pleasure and the emotions of fear lurks Ahriman.

Again, because of man's immaturity Ahriman had to remain concealed; that is, a veil was drawn over his nature. This was done somewhat differently in the case of Lucifer; the external was plunged in *maya* for man, he was deluded into believing that, in place of Ahriman who was lurking everywhere, matter alone existed. Wherever man dreams of matter, there in reality is Ahriman. And the atomic theory of physics is grossly misleading for the material atoms are simply the forces of Ahriman.

Now humanity as a whole is in process of developing, of

evolving, and this evolution is such that in future man will develop more and more his intellectual powers, intellectualism. As a consequence his head will assume a different form externally. In a certain respect this development towards intellectualism first began at the time of the birth of modern natural science, approximately from the sixteenth century onwards. If increasing emphasis is laid upon this intellectual development it will exercise a profound influence upon the Self and the astral body of man. Now in the sixteenth century the traditions of ancient clairvoyance still survived and were contemporaneous with the birth of modern science. People knew that a time would come when, through the higher development of the Self and the astral body, men would be able to see Ahriman more and more clearly. Then, because at first intellectual development was firmly opposed to the perception of the spiritual, a spiritual darkness set in. But by placing the figure of Mephistopheles, who is none other than Ahriman, beside Faust, the sixteenth century was able to show that, fundamentally, Ahriman will become more and more dangerous to the future development of mankind and mankind will be aware of this; that Mephistopheles will become increasingly a kind of seducer of the human race. At first men were aware of this because they still preserved a memory of the ancient spiritual configurations. But mankind as a whole has now forgotten this, but in future man will always be aware that throughout his waking life he is accompanied by Ahriman-Mephistopheles. We must not forget of course the obverse of the medal, namely, that man is moving towards a future when, every time he awakens, he will have the impression, at first like a fleeting dream, but subsequently ever more clearly, that his companion during the night was Lucifer.

From this you can see that, through the occult development of the Self and the astral body, we can anticipate what will befall mankind in the future; we can divine something of the comradeship between Ahriman and Lucifer. In accordance with a definite law of evolution Lucifer first made contact with man during the Lemurian epoch, then, later, as a consequence of the

LECTURE NINE

Luciferic influence, came the influence of Ahriman. In future this situation will be reversed; the Ahrimanic influence will be strong at first and subsequently the Luciferic influence will be associated with it. The Ahrimanic influence will act principally in the waking condition, the Luciferic principally during sleep, or in conditions akin to sleep, but conscious, for conditions of clairvoyant consciousness will develop more and more in the human soul.

Thus man at first needed protection against Ahriman, because Ahriman is destined to enter into man's external sensible life during his waking condition. These protective impulses have been given in the course of human evolution many, many centuries before the corresponding danger was apparent. Whilst today mankind as a whole is not yet fully conscious of Ahriman-Mephistopheles, the protective impulse was manifested at the beginning of our era with the physical incarnation of Christ in the evolution of the earth. Christ's incarnation in the physical body was a precautionary measure to ensure that man might be armed, through receiving the Christ impulse, against the necessary influence which will come from Ahriman-Mephistopheles. When later the Luciferic influence is present, an influence that belongs to another consciousness, man will be armed against it thanks to the appearance of Christ in the etheric body; we have often spoken of this future manifestation and said that it is drawing near. Just as Christ once appeared in the physical body and from that time His impulse has spread far and wide, so from the twentieth century onward He will be seen in an etheric form, at first by a few and then by an ever increasing number. Thus we see how the progressive development of man is brought about by a kind of equilibrium, a kind of balancing of the two impulses. The story of the temptation, Christ's rejection of Lucifer and Ahriman portrayed in different ways by the evangelists – I have spoken of this on a previous occasion[1] – is a sign that through the Christ impulse, through the Mystery of Golgotha, man will be able to find the right path of development in the future. It is part of the true development of the Self and the astral body of man that in this transformed Self and astral body he can receive the impressions of the parts played by Ahriman, Lucifer and Christ in human evolution; a correct development of the Self and the astral body will lead to this knowledge of the three impulses which determine the evolution of mankind.

If we are to develop along the right lines we must overcome the egoity of the astral body in favour of the general interests of mankind and the world. If a person introduces personal interest and aspirations into those regions of his clairvoyant observation where only interests common to mankind and the world ought to claim his attention, it acts like a poison. He does not arrive at the truth, he is the victim of false Imaginations which are simply the reflections of his personal interest and aspirations. It may sometimes happen that a clairvoyant who is still identified with personal interests and aspirations reacts in the following way. I recently received a letter in which someone wrote that he wished to communicate something which I ought to know. He said that Christ had been reincarnated in a physical body and that his address was somewhere in West London; that Mary had been reincarnated in a physical body and her address was that of his niece in such and such a street. Paul also had been reincarnated and was his brother-in-law and his address was also given. Thus all those mentioned in the New Testament had been reincarnated amongst his relations, and their various addresses were given. I could show the letter to anyone who is interested; it is a document, grotesque as it may appear, showing the effects of introducing personal interests into the higher spheres where only the interests of the world and humanity should prevail.

Now we must clearly understand that when someone errs in matters relating to abstract, intellectual knowledge, this error fundamentally is something that can easily be controlled, something that can be comparatively quickly cleared up, although human knowledge has that terrible tendency which I indicated in the last lecture. Because man's knowledge as expressed in our daily waking life includes such diluted impulses that everyone is completely free in relation to these impulses, no one therefore need allow himself to be dazzled by the follies and stupidities of the human intellect, and those who nevertheless allow themselves to be blinded by these follies can be cured in a relatively short time.

Let us suppose that clairvoyant observation leads to false Imaginations in the manner already described; these false Imaginations then infect the soul to such an extent that they stifle sound common sense and intelligence. Thus they do harm to a far greater extent than the merely intellectual absurdities. We must endeavour to imbue everything we have acquired in the field of occultism with the rules of sound common sense; this is the right approach. But if we simply communicate Imaginations without attempting to explain them, as we have tried to do in these lectures – certain occultists will communicate false Imaginations without explaining them – then we suppress in others precisely that critical faculty which should hasten to reject such Imaginations. And it might very well be that, whilst he who perpetrates intellectual absurdities easily invites criticism, he who spreads false Imaginations takes away from those who have confidence in him the power to criticise, that is, he blinds them to the need to reject the Imaginations in question. From this we can see that the moment knowledge oversteps the limits fixed in the natural course of evolution, the moment man raises himself to clairvoyant knowledge, it is absolutely necessary that his development should be directed to the common interests of mankind and the world. This is what has always been recognised in true occultism. And to maintain the contrary, that a sound entry into the spiritual worlds, that is to say, a sound development of the astral body and the Self might be possible without extending human interests to embrace the selfless interests of the world and mankind, to maintain the opposite of what has been stated here, this could only spring from a frivolous attitude to occultism. We must not lose sight of the importance of these things when speaking of the transformations which take place in the astral body and the Self in the course of higher spiritual development.

LECTURE TEN

The Hague, 29 March 1913

We have seen that when esoteric or occult development is pursued in earnest the four principal members of the human being undergo modifications, and you will have observed that in the description we gave we emphasised especially the inner transformation of these four members of human nature, the transformation which is experienced inwardly. We must distinguish clearly between this transformation experienced inwardly and the description of this transformation which is visible externally to the eye of the clairvoyant and which, of course, is something different. In true esoteric development it is important to know first of all what takes place in the inner life of man and what is to be expected when he undergoes an esoteric development. Interesting, though not so important perhaps, is the transformation which is visible externally to the clairvoyant. To sum up briefly, we can say that what is perceived inwardly as a kind of increasing mobility and independence of the different parts of the body manifests itself to the clairvoyant vision, which does not experience the modifications of the physical body from within, but sees them from without, as if the physical body of a person undergoing esoteric development were divided or disjoined, so to speak, and because of this dissociation gives the impression to clairvoyant vision that it is disintegrating. To the clairvoyant eye the physical body of a person who is progressively advancing in occult development is actually seen to grow. If we are concerned with someone who is undergoing a true occult development we notice that when we meet him at a particular moment in his development the physical body, seen by clairvoyant vision at this moment, has a certain dimension; if we meet him again years later his physical body has grown, it has become perceptibly larger. There is therefore a growth of the physical body beyond the normal physical size, but at the same time it becomes more nebulous. Thus, if the person in question has continued to develop, his physical body is seen to become increasingly larger; it consists, so to speak, of separate parts and these individual parts appear in a form which is called in occultism Imagination. The physical body of a person undergoing occult development appears increasingly as an aggregate of Imaginations, of inner pictures that are in a sense living and active, and these pictures are or become ever more interesting, for they are not fortuitous. When the person in question is in the early stage of his occult development they are not particularly significant at first, and they are least of all significant when the clairvoyant vision observes the body of a person who has not yet developed occultly.

In the latter case we perceive at first a number of pictures, of Imaginations. To the clairvoyant vision the physical substance disappears and is replaced by Imaginations; but these are so compressed that, instead of showing the pleasing, inwardly radiant aspect of a person pursuing occult development, they manifest as opaque substance. Even in the case of the person who is not yet developed they can be seen, namely as parts, and each part is related to something in the macrocosm. Fundamentally one can distinguish twelve members, each of which is really a picture – a picture of one part of the cosmos. When all twelve members are united one has the impression that some unknown painter has painted miniatures of the macrocosm, twelve in number, and from these has formed the physical human body. Now when the person is undergoing occult development this picture becomes progressively larger, but at the same time inwardly more pleasing, ever more luminous. This is because, in the case of the person who is not engaged in occult development, the macrocosm is reflected only in its physical aspect, whilst in the case of the person who is undergoing occult training the pictures reveal more and more the spiritual content, they are pictures of the spiritual Beings of the macrocosm. Thus occult development also shows us that the person pursuing occult development passes from a purely physical microcosm to a more and more spiritual microcosm, that is, he reflects more and more the pictures not only of planets and suns, but also of entities belonging to the higher Hierarchies. This is the difference between the persons engaged in occult training and those who are indifferent to such training. The more a person advances in occult development the more the higher Hierarchies are revealed to him. Thus we come to know the structure of the world by observing clairvoyantly the physical body of man.

The etheric body of a person who is not following an occult training shows the course of the earth's evolution, that which is successive in time; it shows how planets and suns, human civilisation on earth or individual human beings are transformed in the course of their incarnations, how they appear in the successive stages of their development. The etheric body is therefore a recorder, it records the story of the course of the earth's evolution. Whilst the physical body of man resembles a collection of pictures painted by an unknown hand, the etheric body shows itself to be a kind of recorder which records the inner happenings of cosmic history itself. The further a person advances in occult development, the further his insights react back in time. The etheric body of a person who has made relatively little progress in occult development shows to clairvoyant vision perhaps only the physical inheritance of a few preceding generations – for this development is also shown in the etheric body of man. The more advanced the occult development of a person, the more possible it becomes to see in his etheric body the record of civilisations, the particular incarnations of various individualities, indeed to reach back to the genesis of the cosmos and to grasp the part played by the Spirits of the higher Hierarchies in the birth of the cosmos.

To ordinary observation the astral body can only be perceived through its inner reflection, through experiences of thought, will and feeling; it becomes more and more an expression of the value of man's inner being in the cosmos. I want you to attach particular importance to this description. The astral body of a person undergoing occult development becomes more and more the expression of his value in the cosmos. In an earlier lecture we described how we arrive at the knowledge that the astral body in its original nature is a kind of egoist, that this egoism has to be overcome in occult development by transforming our personal interests into universal interests. If we observe the astral body of a person engaged in higher development we shall know, according to whether it appears dark or opaque, or is inwardly clear and luminous, according to whether it betrays itself in shrill dissonances or pleasing harmonies, whether the person in question is still attached to his personal interest of which we have already spoken, or whether he has really made the interests of the world his own. The astral body of a person pursuing higher development whose development has followed a strictly correct moral course reveals how estimable man becomes when he extends the horizon of his interests from the personal to the universal-human, to the universal concerns of mankind. The astral becomes ever more radiant, more luminous when man learns to make the affairs of mankind in general and of the world at large more and more his personal concern.

As man progresses further in his development his Self shows increasingly a tendency to divide, to become dissociated. It projects externally, as it were, the contents of its consciousness and these contents it diffuses over the world. If, for example, a person wishes to know a Being of the Hierarchy of the Angels, the ordinary forces of cognition will not suffice for this purpose. If he really wishes to know this Being he must be able to transfer his consciousness, that is, he must be able to separate the forces of his Self and transfer a part of his Self-consciousness to the entity of the Angelic Being in question. Whatever Being we wish to know, we can only do so by transferring our Self-consciousness to this Being. Our Self feels an impulse to go out of itself and to transfer itself to the other Being and allow to live in the other Being that which at first lived only in the Self. At a lower stage of development, at the level of ordinary existence, this impulse manifests itself in a desire to be released from waking consciousness, in the need for sleep. And that which psychically impels man to sleep is the same impulse which in higher development directs his consciousness, not into the unconscious world of sleep, but into the consciousness of the Angeloi or Spirits of Form or still higher Hierarchies. Thus one might ask the paradoxical question: What is the significance of learning to know one of the Elohim? It means to be sufficiently developed that one is able to enter into the consciousness of the Elohim during sleep and to awaken in the Elohim with the awareness of this Spirit of Form, of this Spirit of the higher Hierarchies. To know a higher Being means to surrender our consciousness as we do in sleep, but to surrender it in such a way that, thanks to the higher forces awakened in us, this consciousness reawakens and radiates towards us as the consciousness of this higher Being.

Thus, in true occult development, an astral body resembles a sun which radiates its world interests. A Self, however, that attains higher development resembles the planets which revolve round the sun of the astral body and which, on their path through the cosmos meet other Beings and by meeting them bring tidings of these other Beings to the neophyte in search of knowledge. Thus the astral body and the Self of the person undergoing occult development present, in fact, the picture of a sun (which is the astral body) surrounded by its planets which are so many multiplications of the Self projected into other Beings in order that through that which his multiplied Self reflects back to him from these other entities, man may know their nature.

And the feeling we have when we are aware of the inner nature of these members of the higher Hierarchies (we learn to recognise them externally through the physical and etheric bodies, and to recognise them inwardly through the astral body and the Self, through these bodies we come in touch with these Beings of the higher Hierarchies) the feeling we have is as though we had to make our astral body into a sun and to detach from ourselves a Self which has the capacity to penetrate into the

LECTURE TEN

Hierarchy of the Angels; another Self which could penetrate into the Hierarchy of the Archangels, another into the Hierarchy of the Spirits of Form, a fourth into the Hierarchy of the Spirits of Movement, a fifth into the Hierarchy of the Spirits of Wisdom and of Will, a sixth Self into the Hierarchy of the Cherubim and a seventh into that of the Seraphim. It is possible that when a person develops the four members of his being to a higher stage, he attains to the experience we have just described. This is possible; but in addition to this development of the Self in the manner I have just indicated, he can attain to a still higher development of the Self.

Because the Self detaches seven Selves from itself, the eighth Self which remains behind undergoes, as a consequence, a higher development. Let us consider the matter in the following way: We have the original Self with which man is endowed before his occult development. He undergoes occult development and can then project seven Selves out of himself; in order that the Self originally given him has been able to project seven Selves he has been obliged to make use of an inner force, with the result that the Self has risen one stage higher. Now I beg you to bear in mind that the process which I have here described in a radical fashion takes place gradually. The person undergoing occult development does not of course become immediately in his astral body a perfect sun surrounded by the planets of his Selves; he attains at first to an imperfect sun existence, to imperfect developments of his planetary Selves. This is a gradual process; and at the same time the development of the normal Self into a higher Self takes place slowly and gradually. When this development has reached a certain stage, when therefore the Self actually reaches ever higher stages, then gradually the possibility arises of looking back to former incarnations. This is the stage when the Self rises beyond itself, when the Self overcomes itself thanks to the forces which at the same time enabled it to understand the higher Hierarchies. We could say therefore that, to clairvoyant vision, with regard to his Self and astral body, man becomes star-like, akin to a stellar system thanks to his occult development.

I have now described to you more or less what is revealed to external clairvoyance, to the perception of a person who is becoming clairvoyant, whereas in the previous lectures I described more the inner experiences. I have still something important to add which will amplify in some measure an indication already given. When man develops his astral body and his Self he is able to perceive, as you know, a world that was previously empty now filled with the Beings of the higher Hierarchies – Angels, Archangels, Archai and so on. You may now raise the question: Do the kingdoms of nature also change? Yes indeed they change quite considerably. I said, as you will remember, that to the clairvoyant the physical body of the ordinary person appears as an ensemble of pictures which, the more the person progresses, become inwardly increasingly more luminous.

And what is the position of the animals? To clairvoyant vision the physical body of the animals is also transformed into Imaginations, and then we know that these animals are not what they appear to be in the world of *maya*; they are Imaginations, that is, they are Imaginations seen through a human consciousness who then conceives the animals as Imaginations. Who evokes these Imaginations? Animals, plants also in their external forms – but plants less than animals and minerals least of all – are Imaginations belonging to Ahriman. Our physicists try to discover physical laws in the external kingdoms of nature; the occultist realises more and more that the external kingdoms of nature, in so far as they appear as material entities, are Imaginations of Ahriman. Now we know that behind the animals are the Group Souls. The Group Souls are not Imaginations of Ahriman; it is only the individual animals in their external forms that are Imaginations of Ahriman. The Group Soul of the lion species, for example, belongs so to speak to the good spiritual Beings and in the war that Ahriman wages against these spiritual Beings he presses their Group Soul into the individual animal forms and imprints upon them his own Imaginations. The individual lions actually existing on earth are projected out of the Group Soul by Ahriman. Thus the environment also is in process of gradual transformation into something totally different from its appearance in the world of *maya*.

In order that you may have a systematic guide to the thoughts to which this lecture cycle has introduced us, I will draw you a diagram.

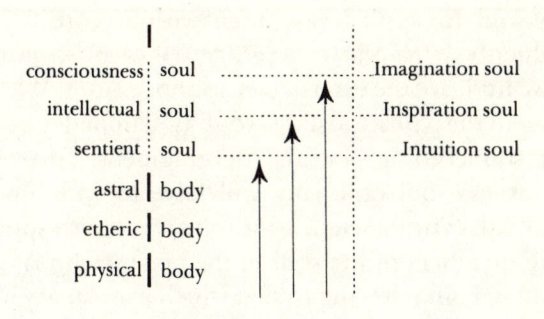

```
               |
  consciousness : soul    ............:...Imagination soul
    intellectual : soul             ↑  :....Inspiration soul
       sentient : soul    .........↑....:......Intuition soul
         astral | body         ↑
        etheric | body
       physical | body
```

First, I will indicate here on the left what we may call the structure of the ordinary human constitution: physical body, etheric body, astral body, sentient soul, intellectual or mind soul, consciousness soul, Spirit Self, Life Spirit and Spirit Man. Such is the constitution of man. I will represent this by a broken line. The soul life includes the sentient soul, next the intellectual soul, then the consciousness soul, and then the Spirit Self. The higher members we can take for granted since we do not need to consider them today. This constitution of man manifests itself externally in such a way that the corporeal element is experienced in the three lower members, the psychic element in the three middle members, and the Spirit Self is only present in man as a pointer to the future. When a person undergoes spiritual development it is important at first to suppress certain things in the soul itself. We have seen that it is particularly important that the individual should exclude external sense impressions. That is the first condition of true occult progress. By excluding external sensory impressions the principle of the soul that is developed chiefly under the influence of external sense impressions, namely the consciousness soul, is inwardly transformed. Remember that the consciousness soul at the present time has reached maximum development because it relies largely upon external sense impressions. The fact that the consciousness soul is inwardly fortified to a large extent by the impressions received through the senses must not be confused with the fact that these sense impressions are mediated by the sentient soul. In occult development we must consider which are the influences that most strengthen the consciousness soul; these, we find, are the external sense impressions. When they are eliminated the consciousness soul is damped down; in the person undergoing occult development, therefore, the consciousness soul especially will have to withdraw into the background. (On the right I indicate what corresponds to the separate members of the soul in the person who is developing spiritually.) I am referring to that which in ordinary life induces a person to emphasise his Ego, to affirm his Ego especially in every possible domain. In the present epoch the Ego asserts itself in the domain of thought. We incessantly hear: this is my point of view, this is what I think. As if it mattered what X or Y thinks; as if it were not far more important to discover where the truth lies. No matter what a person may think it is a proven fact that the sum of the three angles of a triangle is 180°. Counting from man upwards it is incontrovertible that the Hierarchies fall into three groups of three and man's point of view is immaterial. The affirmation of the Ego then withdraws into the background and in its place the consciousness soul, whose principal purpose originally had been to cultivate the Ego, is gradually filled with what we call Imagination. We can say therefore that in the person who is developing spiritually the consciousness soul is transformed into the *Imagination Soul*.

We also know from the indications given in the earlier lectures that thinking itself, which is developed principally in the intellectual or mind soul, must also be transformed. We were told that thinking must desist more and more from developing its own thoughts, that it must suppress personal thoughts more and more, that the human personality must eradicate independent thinking. When man succeeds in suppressing the experiences of his intellectual or mind soul in his ordinary life, then his normal thinking, good sense and also his ordinary affective life on the physical plane are replaced by Inspiration. The intellectual or mind soul is transformed into the Inspirational or *Inspiration Soul*. The inspired works of culture have been in-spired into, breathed into the transformed intellectual soul.

The sentient soul especially is gradually eliminated when we overcome the astral body, when we make the world interests our own and surmount more and more our personal feelings. The sentient soul is thereby transformed, all the inner impulses, inner passions and emotions are changed into Intuitions, and in place of the sentient soul appears the *Intuition Soul*. Here on the right (see diagram, p. 147) we can indicate the person who has developed spiritually; we can say of him that he consists of astral body, etheric body and physical body, but inwardly of the Intuition Soul, the Inspiration Soul and the Imagination Soul which passes over into Spirit Self. And from this diagram which gives the true facts of occult observation you may gather from these lectures that a person influences his occult development by the degree of his moral development. A man who is still the victim of his personal emotions and passions, who acts under the influence, one might say, of human instincts, is still living entirely in his sentient soul; he does not moderate his instincts at the behest of reason, nor by the development of his consciousness. If I indicate moral development by the little arrow in the middle, then he has only developed as far as the sentient soul.

The case may arise therefore where a person has developed only as far as the sentient soul, that is to say, he is dominated entirely by his appetites and impulses. Let us assume that his progress had been accelerated by occult development. The consequence would be that he would have transformed his sentient soul into the Intuition Soul and he would experience certain Intuitions; these Intuitions however would represent simply the transformation of his own impulses, appetites and instincts. A person who, in his moral development, has arrived at the intellectual soul, i.e. who has acquired clear-cut, more universal ideas, whose mind embraces the general interests of the world, such a person will at least transform his intellectual or mind soul into the Inspiration Soul. He is able to arrive at certain inspirations although his clairvoyant vision is still not wholly unclouded.

It is only when a person has penetrated with his Ego as far as the consciousness soul that he is able to transform his consciousness soul into the Imagination Soul; the rest follows as a matter of course because he has already passed through the other stages. In our epoch therefore the purpose of a clairvoyant appropriate to this age must be to set man the task of cultivating his moral development so that he divests first of all his impulses and desires of the personal element and raises them to the level where his personal interests become world interests; then he must endeavour really to understand himself as an Ego, but as an Ego in the consciousness soul. Then the sentient soul, the intellectual soul and the consciousness soul can safely be transformed into the Intuition Soul, the Inspiration Soul and the Imagination Soul. When we observe ordinary consciousness on

the physical plane we find that it is the sentient soul which is the richest soul. Though this soul be never so lowly, how many instincts and impulses are concealed within it! Of what impulses and desires is it not capable! The content of the intellectual or mind soul is poorer in emotional response, but poorest of all is the consciousness soul which is limited to the consciousness of the Self, reduced, so to speak, to a point. One could say that the figure which represents the human soul in its natural condition on the physical plane would be a pyramid, at the base the sum total of impulses, desires and passions, at the apex, the point of consciousness. An inverted pyramid represents the developed soul of the true clairvoyant; here the base represents all kinds of Imaginations which can be formed and which express everything that can reveal the contents of the Cosmos; the inverted apex represents the higher individual consciousness of man. This diagram serves to a certain extent as a yardstick in a further sense. In the new edition of my book *Theosophy* I have already indicated that the sentient soul is, as it were, the provisionally transformed astral body. We can therefore sum up as follows: Below is the physical body, then the etheric body, then the astral body. The provisionally transformed astral body is the sentient soul on the physical plane; the provisionally transformed etheric body is the intellectual or mind soul and the provisionally transformed physical body is the consciousness soul.

astral body	sentient soul	–	Intuition Soul
etheric body	intellectual soul	–	Inspiration Soul
physical body	consciousness soul	–	Imagination Soul

Thus in our present cycle of humanity the consciousness soul is first localised in the physical body, that is to say, it makes use of the physical organs. The intellectual soul is situated in the etheric body which means that it makes use of the etheric movements. The sentient soul containing impulses, desires and passions uses the forces localised in the astral body. The intellectual or mind soul which contains the forces of inner feeling, of sympathy or compassion, makes use of the etheric body; and the consciousness soul makes use of the brain of the physical body.

When as described the sentient soul is transformed into the Intuition Soul, you must also imagine correspondingly that the Intuition Soul uses the astral body of man as its instrument. The Inspiration Soul is the transmuted intellectual or mind soul, its instrument is the etheric body of man. And the Imagination Soul, the transformed consciousness soul, has as its instrument the physical body of man. If you now compare the scheme shown here with what I said earlier, you will realise that this scheme is a memory picture. I said in effect that to clairvoyant vision the physical body is transformed into Imaginations which are pictures of the macrocosm. In the diagram, the Imagination Soul fills the physical body; it actually enters into the physical body and permeates it so that the clairvoyant consciousness, the more it meets a developed human being, sees the members of the physical body to be permeated with ever loftier Imaginations which are impressed into the physical body by the inner being of this personality. In the ordinary person are to be found a number of Imaginations which are imprinted into the members of his physical body by higher spiritual Beings; in the more highly developed man, other Imaginations are added to the already existing Imaginations and these he imprints into the members of his body from his own inner being, so that the organs of the physical body of a person who has developed spiritually become progressively richer.

In this scheme I wanted to give you a brief statement which sums up what I have described more fully in these lectures. I wish especially to draw your attention to the fact that, thanks to this scheme, you will always be able to remember that the sentient soul, the intellectual or mind soul, and the consciousness soul are transformed, so that the consciousness soul does not become the Intuition Soul, but the Imagination Soul; and the sentient soul does not become the Imagination Soul, but the Intuition Soul.

Thus we have a sketch of what I wished to say in the course of these lectures on this subject: the transformations of the human sheaths and of the human Self in the course of spiritual development seriously undertaken or in the course of an esoteric-occult development – which is fundamentally the same thing. We began, as you will have observed, with the slight, almost imperceptible modifications of the physical body, modifications which the neophyte scarcely perceives at first; the individual members of the physical body become inwardly more and more alive, whilst normally the whole physical body of man alone appears as a living entity. We then saw that certain transformations occur, revealing important facts of the inner life, modifications in the astral body and the Self which evoke those powerful Imaginations through which we can feel ourselves seemingly transposed to the beginning of our terrestrial evolution and even further back – Imaginations which lead to the Paradise Imagination and to the Cain and Abel Imagination. We saw that, in fact, there arises as a reality in the physical body a kind of force which enables it to subdivide, as it were, and yet it remains a whole; it does not yield to this tendency to divide because in our present cycle of humanity occult training may not go so far as to injure the physical body. There is, however, an intensity of occult development that may lead to the stimulation of inwardly destructive forces in the physical body and the etheric body. And this danger always exists when a person meets the Guardian of the Threshold. This meeting is not possible without running the risk of implanting destructive forces in the physical and etheric bodies. But every true occult development provides the necessary remedies at the same time and these are the six supplementary occult exercises which you will find described in my book *Occult Science*: concentration of thought, that is, control of one's thoughts, disciplined organisation of thoughts; development of a certain initiative of will; a certain equanimity in face of joy and sorrow; a positive approach in one's attitude to the world, a certain detachment. He who cultivates these qualities in his soul parallel with his occult development certainly develops in his physical and etheric bodies, under the influence of occult development, a tendency to disintegration, that is, a tendency to assimilate seeds of death. But as this tendency develops it is neutralised and consequently is never really active when a person develops the qualities indicated above, or when, thanks to his moral development, he already has a sufficiency of qualities equivalent to these six qualities.

I have attempted to give you more than a description of occult development; I have endeavoured to awaken in your hearts a feeling of what occult development is, and to show you the many and various ways in which it influences and transforms the human being. You have been able to divine and to feel that when a person pursues occult development he is faced by many shattering experiences and much that is dangerous. But alongside many things that in this theoretical exposition have perhaps awakened a certain dread, we must always bear in mind the thought which dispels all fear, can banish all fear of danger and which evokes in our soul enthusiasm and strength of will – the thought that, by developing ourselves further we are contributing actively in a small measure to the evolution willed by the gods. He who can grasp the full significance of this thought and the enthusiasm it inspires, he who can grasp this thought in such a way that it presents evolution, occult development in its most beautiful sense, as man's duty, he who can feel this, feels already, despite all dangers, all struggles, all confusion, all obstacles the approach of the bliss of the spiritual worlds. When we feel this thought of the power of the ideal of occult development to kindle enthusiasm, we already begin to feel the bliss of the progress realised; but this bliss means that we must recognise this occult progress as a necessity. The future of such spiritual-esoteric movements as ours will depend more and more upon the realisation that the spiritual development of mankind is a necessity. Rejection of, hostility towards spiritual development will signify an affinity with the waste products of the earth which have become atrophied and have abandoned the evolution of the universe willed by the gods.

NOTES

page 40   *Lectures on Anthroposophy in Berlin*: Rudolf Steiner, *The Wisdom of Man, of the Soul and of the Spirit*, 12 lectures given in Berlin, 23–27 October 1909, 1–4 November 1910, 12–16 December 1911, Anthroposophic Press, New York, 1971.

page 53   *Schools of Zarathustra, Amshaspands*: see Rudolf Steiner, *Turning Points in Spiritual History*, lecture on Zarathustra. Rudolf Steiner Publishing Company, London, 1934. Also Rudolf Steiner, *Mythen und Zeichen*, Rudolf Steiner-Nachlassverwaltung, Dornach, 1951.

page 109   *Augustine, Manichean Bishop Faustinus*: the description of the various Faust figures is taken from *Die Entstehung des Volksbuches von Dr. Faust* by Herman Grimm. See also Rudolf Steiner, *Geisteswissenschaftliche Erläuterungen zu Goethes Faust*, Rudolf Steiner-Nachlassverwaltung, Dornach, 1967.

page 115   *Guardian of the Threshold*: see Rudolf Steiner's Mystery Play *The Guardian of the Threshold*, Steiner Book Centre, 1973. Also *The Secrets of the Threshold*, 8 lectures given at Munich, 24–31 August 1913, Anthroposophical Publishing Company, London, 1928.

page 127   *I used to know a poet*: Hermann Rollet (1819–1904). See also Rudolf Steiner, *The Younger Generation*, 13 lectures given in Stuttgart, 3–15 October 1922, Anthroposophic Press, New York, 1967.

page 132   *In an earlier course of lectures*: Rudolf Steiner, *Occult History*, 6 lectures given in Stuttgart, 27 December 1910 – 1 January 1911, lecture 2.

page 137   *I have spoken of this on a previous occasion*: see Rudolf Steiner *The Gospel of St. Matthew*, 12 lectures given at Berne, 1–12 September 1910, Rudolf Steiner Press, London, 1965. Also *The Fifth Gospel*, 7 lectures given in Oslo, 1–6 October 1913, Rudolf Steiner Press, London, 1968. Also *The Mystery of Golgotha*, a lecture given at Oxford on 27 August 1922, Rudolf Steiner Publishing Company, London, 1940.

Some relevant books:

RUDOLF STEINER:
  Knowledge of the Higher Worlds
  Occult Science – An Outline
  A Road to Self-Knowledge and the Threshold
    of the Spiritual World
  Manifestations of Karma
  Overcoming Nervousness
  Supersensible Man

FRANZ E. WINKLER:
  Man – The Bridge between Two Worlds

GUENTHER WACHSMUTH:
  The Evolution of Mankind

KARL KÖNIG:
  The Human Soul

CARL UNGER:
  Principles of Spiritual Science